The Musician's Notebook

Piano

Manuscript Pages for the Inspired Artist

by Matthew Teacher

CIDER MILL PRESS

BOOK PUBLISHERS

Kennebunkport, Maine

ISBN-13: 978-1-60433-331-2
ISBN-10: 1-60433-331-6

This book may be ordered by mail from the publisher. Please include $3.50 for postage and handling.
Please support your local bookseller first!

Books published by Cider mill Press Book Publishers are available at special discounts for bulk purchases in the United States by corporations, institutions, and other organizations.
For more information, please contact the publisher.

Cider Mill Press Book Publishers
"Where good books are ready for press"
12 Port Farm Road
Kennebunkport, Maine 04046

Visit us on the web!
www.cidermillpress.com

Design by Alicia Freile, Tango Media

Printed in China

1 2 3 4 5 6 7 8 9 0

First Edition

The Musician's Notebook: Piano

Now there is one home for all your creative musings — for the songs you carry around in your head (or on random scraps of paper). This is a musician's journal created by a musician for a musician. Use it to bring clarity to your ideas and substance to your vision. Fill your notebook with your greatest licks, motifs, and completed songs. Track chords and riffs and draw inspiration from a collection of quotes by artists who inspire. Within this book there's a home for your creative thoughts. And now they won't get lost! It's all here — *The Musician's Notebook: Piano*. Start using it today.

Illustration Key for Using This Book

Use to label scales and chords

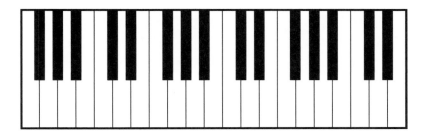

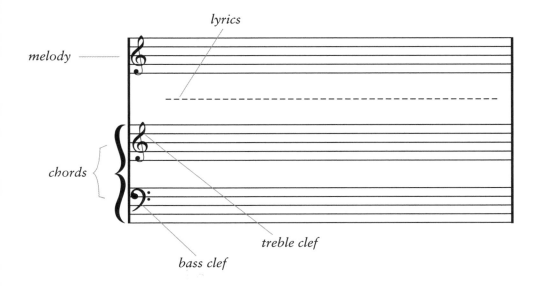

All you need is ears.

GEORGE MARTIN

Title

Author

Date

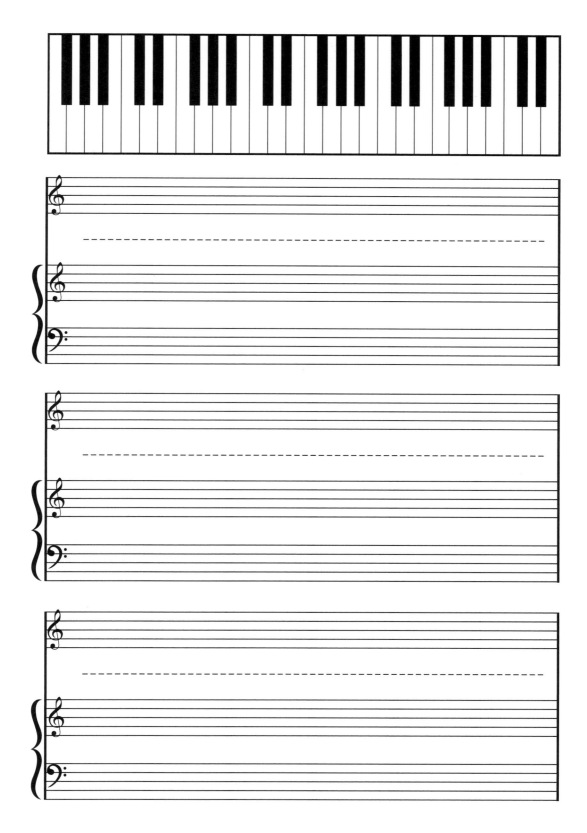

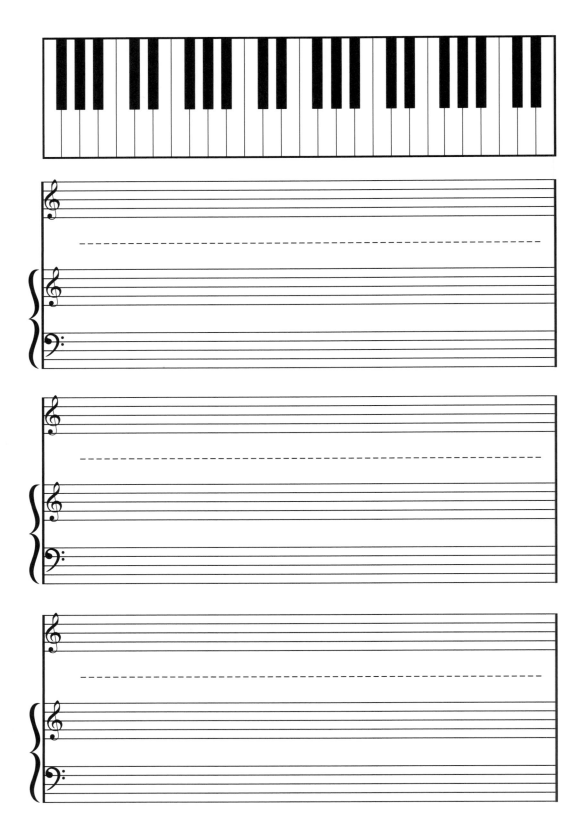

The wise musicians are those who play
what they can master.

DUKE ELLINGTON

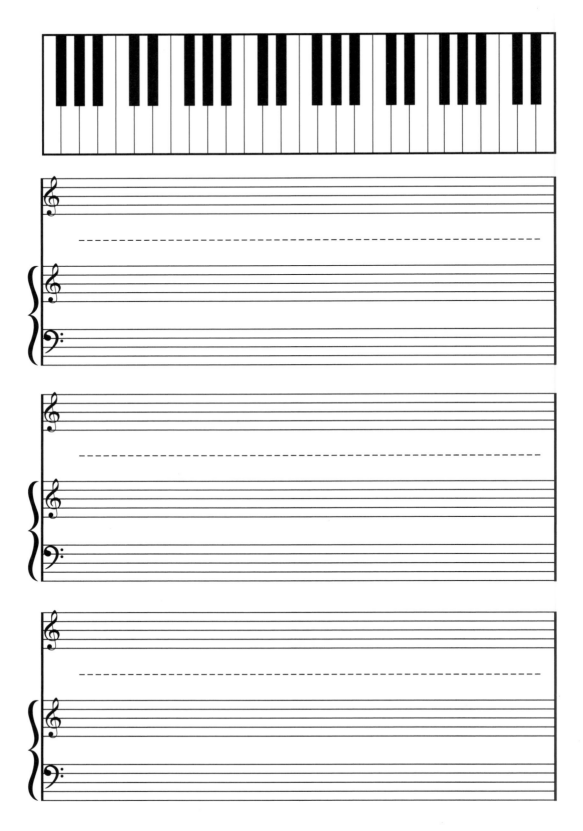

Too many jazz pianists limit themselves to a personal style,
a trademark, so to speak.

OSCAR PETERSON

Title

Author

Date

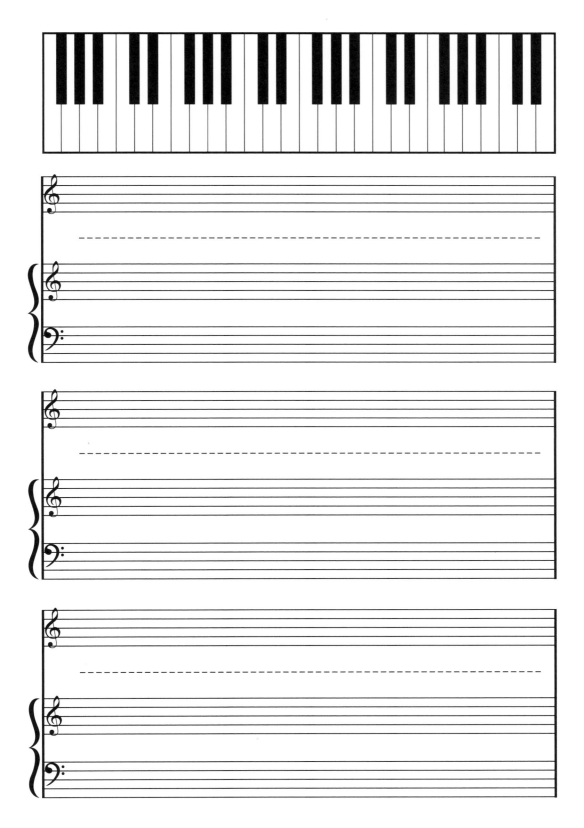

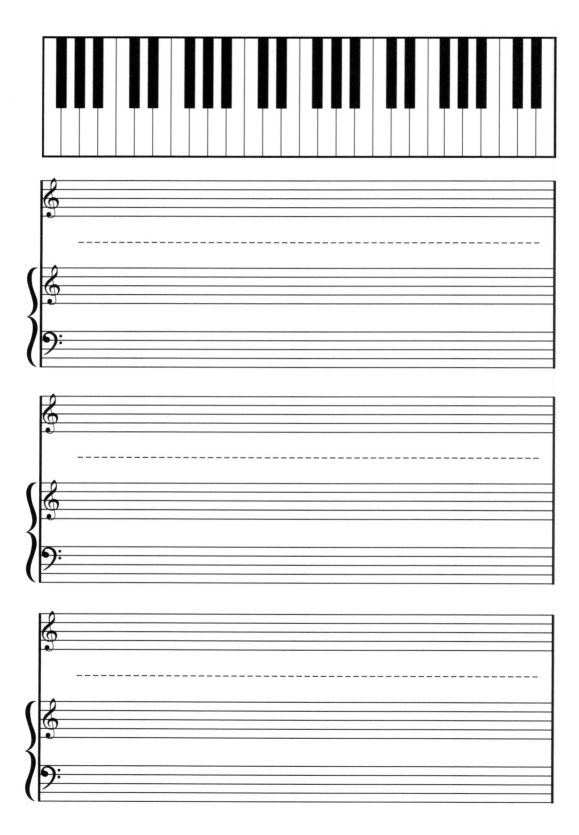

It's easy to play any musical instrument: all you have to do is touch the right key at the right time and the instrument will play itself.

JOHANN SEBASTIAN BACH

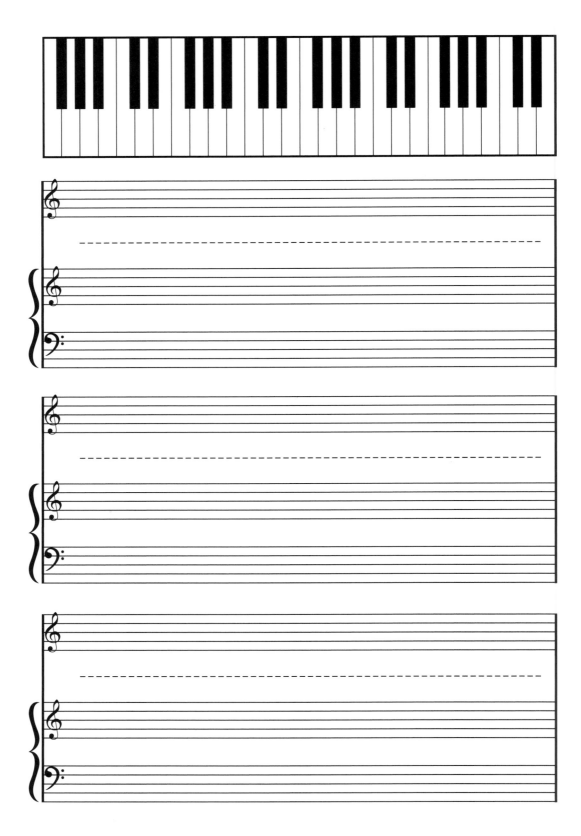

I was considered very good amongst my friends, that is so far as
the writing period. And I've always had a kind of a little inkling
to write a tune at most any place that I would ever land.

JELLY ROLL MORTON

Title

Author

Date

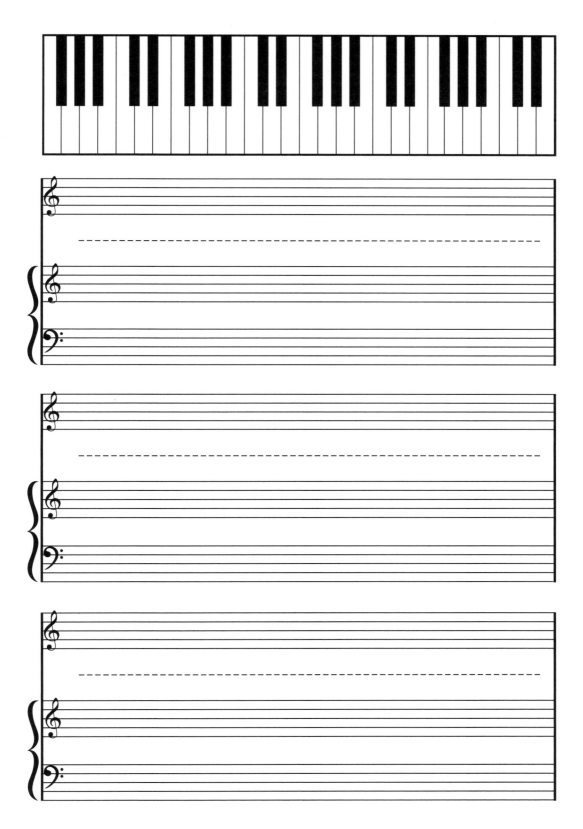

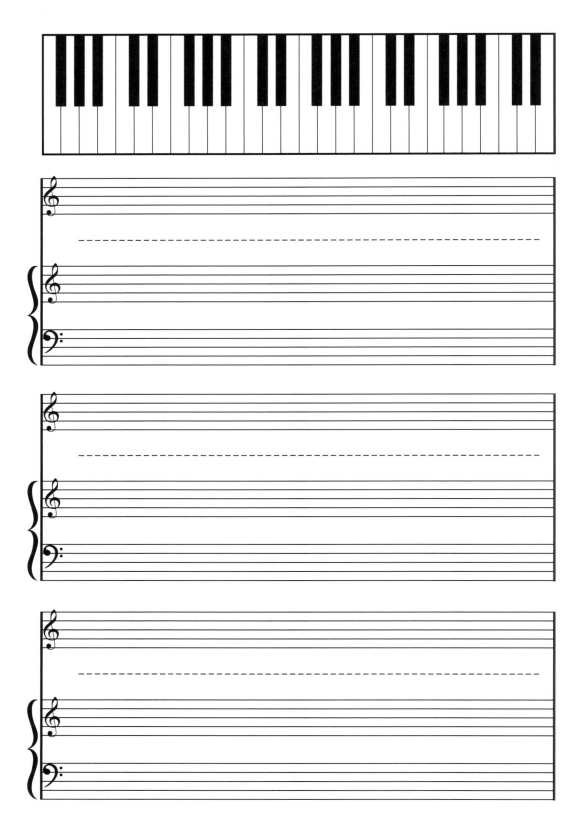

Neither a lofty degree of intelligence nor imagination
nor both together go to the making of genius.
Love, love, love, that is the soul of genius.

WOLFGANG AMADEUS MOZART

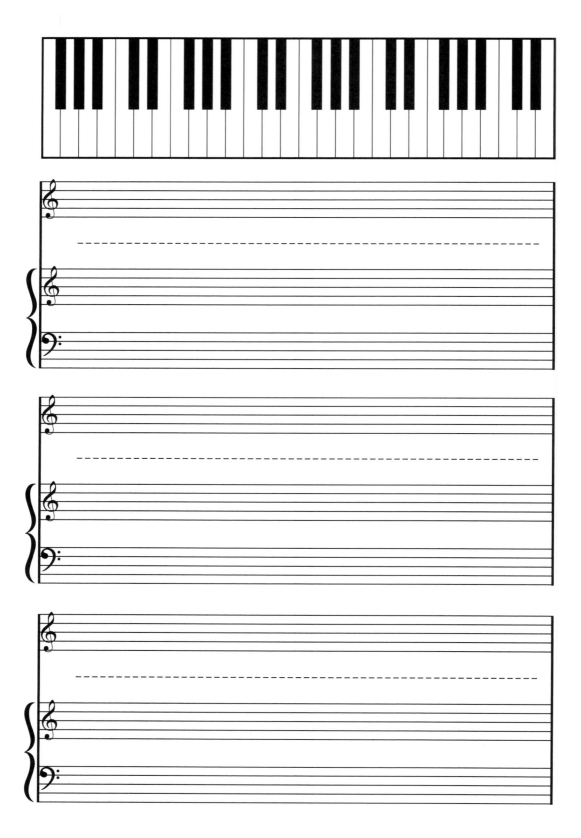

Musically, I always allow myself to jump off of cliffs. At least that's what it feels like to me. Whether that's what it actually sounds like might depend on what the listener brings to the songs.

TORI AMOS

Title _____

Author _____

Date _____

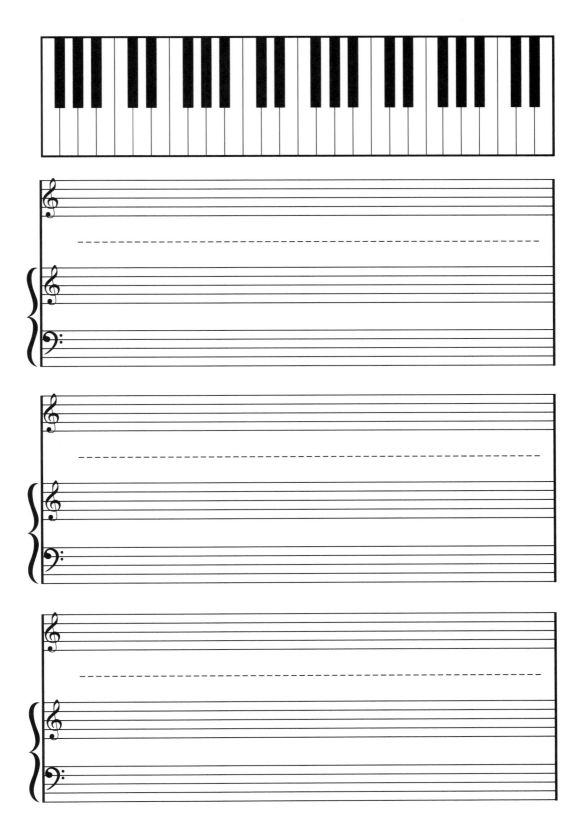

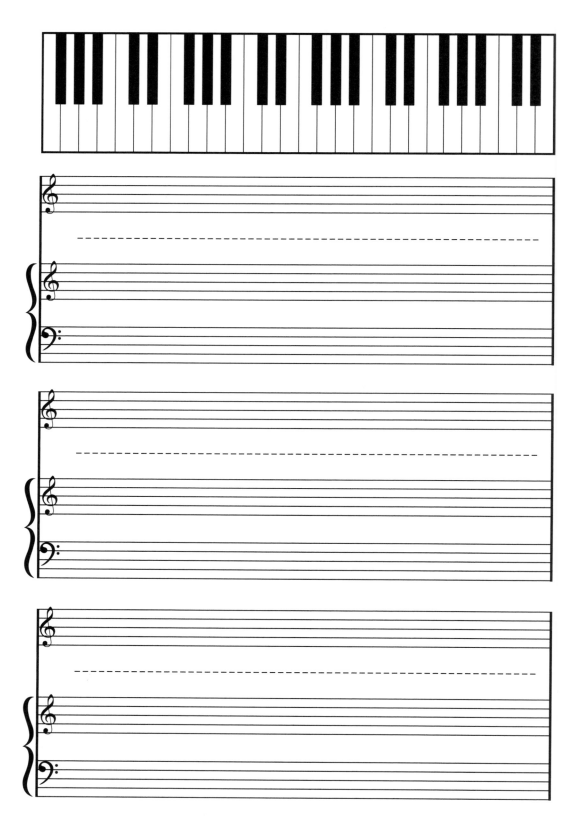

I, of course, wanted to play real jazz. When we played pop tunes, and naturally we had to, I wanted those pops to kick! Not loud and fast, understand, but smoothly and with a definite punch.

COUNT BASIE

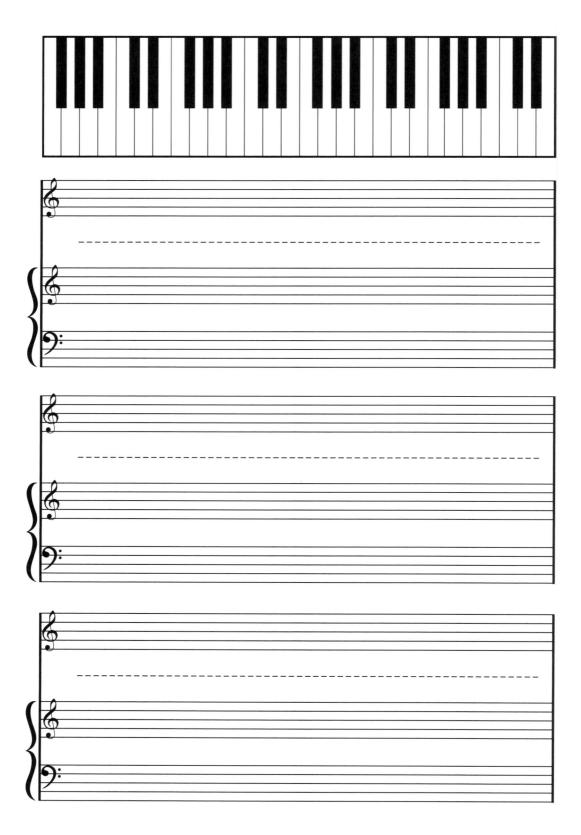

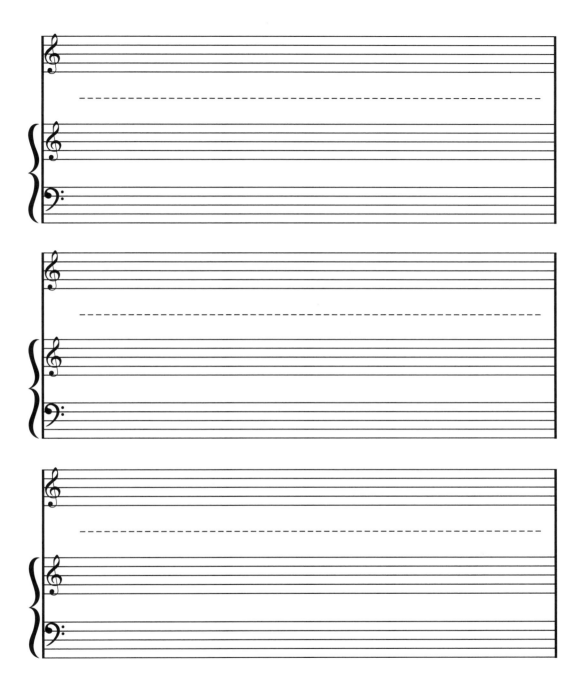

Music is the greatest communication in the world. Even if people don't understand the language that you're singing in, they still know good music when they hear it.

LOU RAWLS

Title _____

Author _____

Date _____

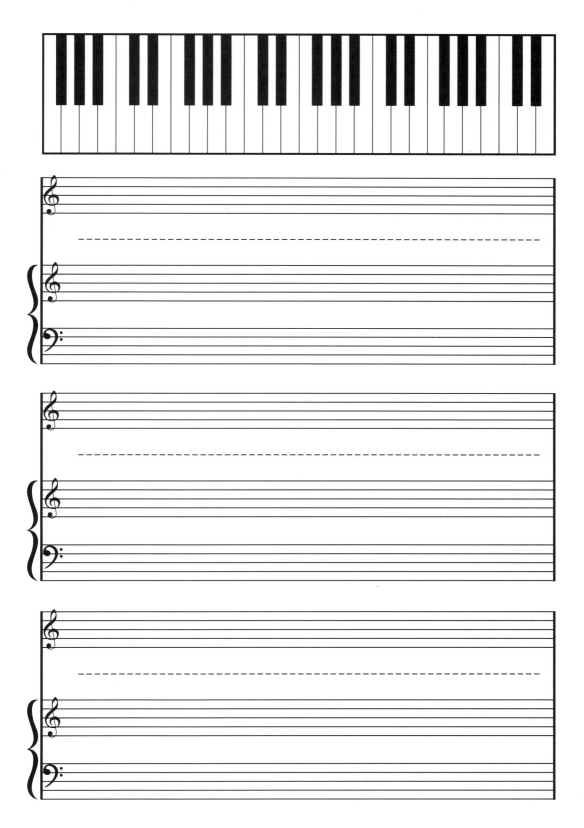

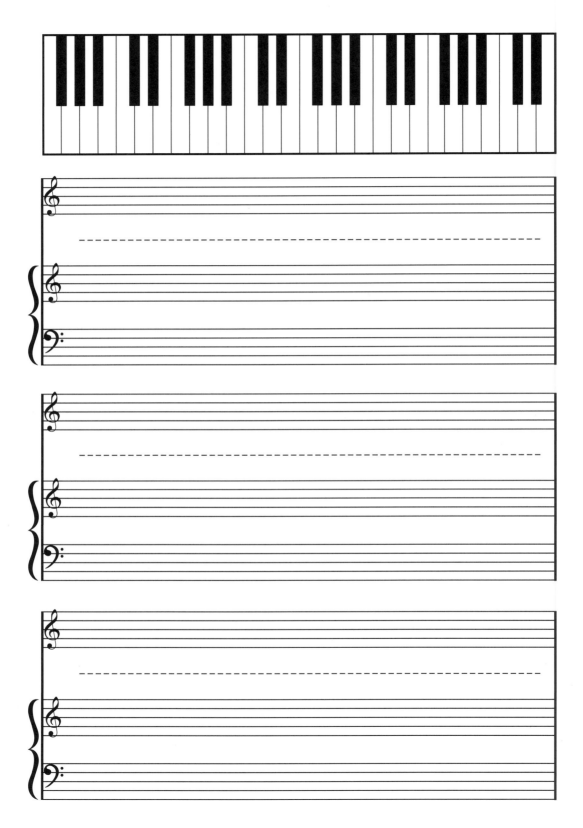

I don't try to sound like anyone but me anymore.
If something is out of my element, I try to avoid it.

NORAH JONES

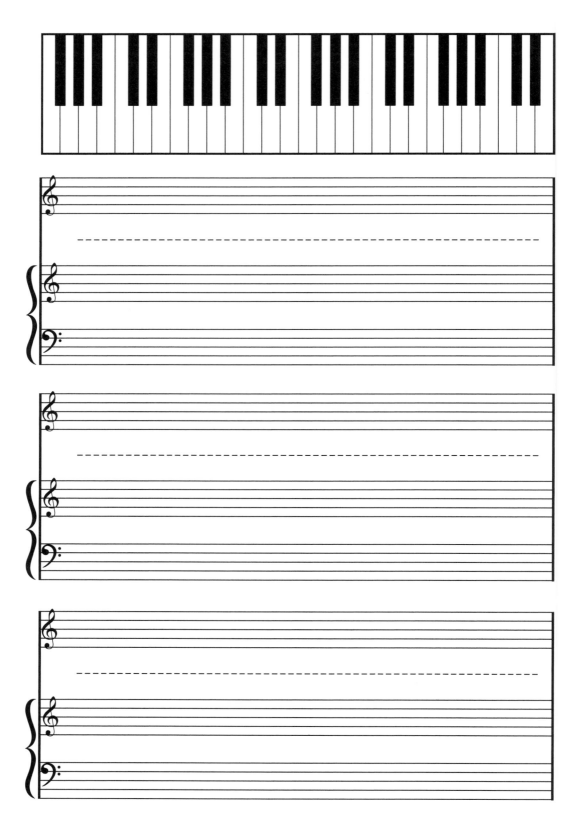

I'm sort of still a bit stuck to that convention of writing a song with a four-line verse, the more traditional phrasing of a stanza.

SARAH MCLACHLAN

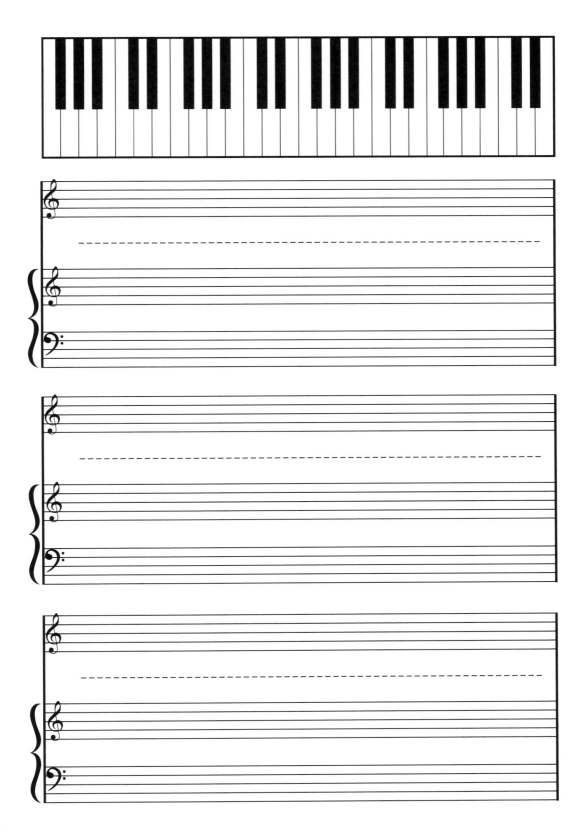

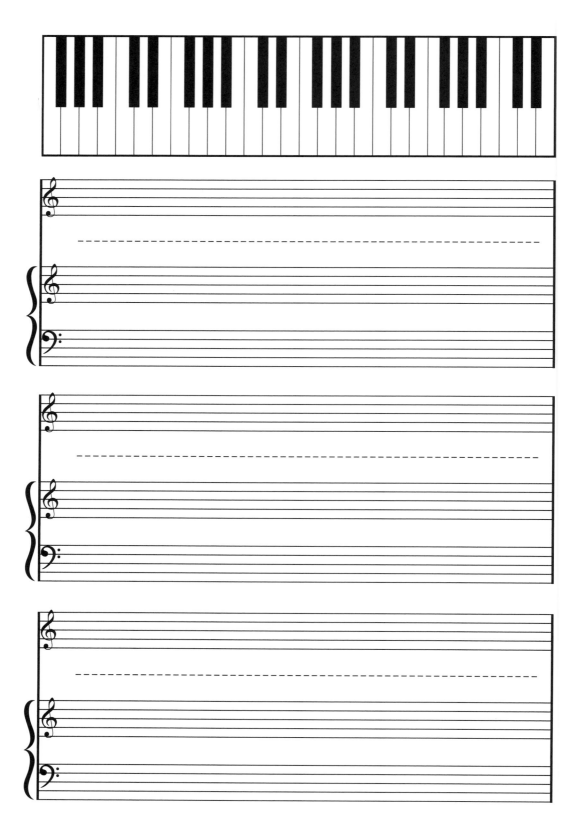

I start songs all the time. If I weren't so lazy, I would finish them.
It's like when I have a deadline I have to meet. I always feel very
lucky that I am forced to make records at certain times.

BEN FOLDS

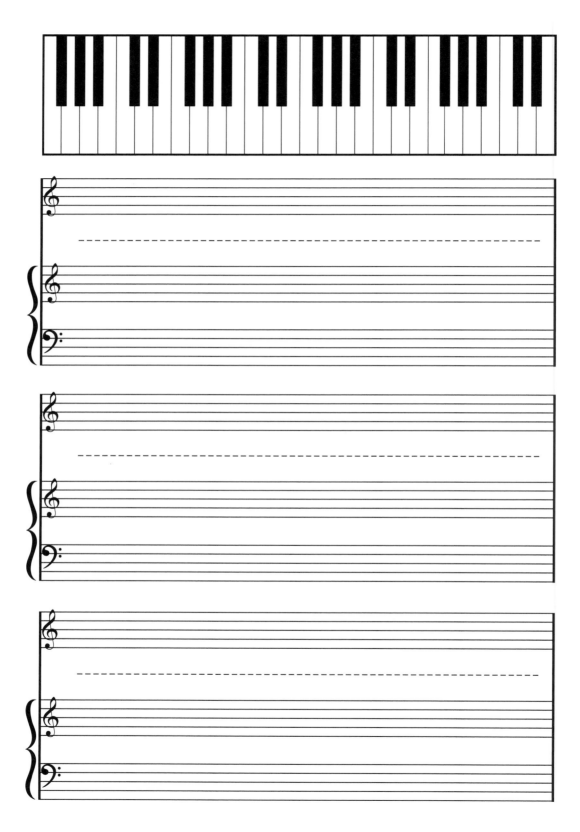

And I just practiced on it and practiced on it.
I found a lot of little things about details, about accents
and how much of an accent to make.

HERBIE HANCOCK

Title _____

Author _____

Date _____

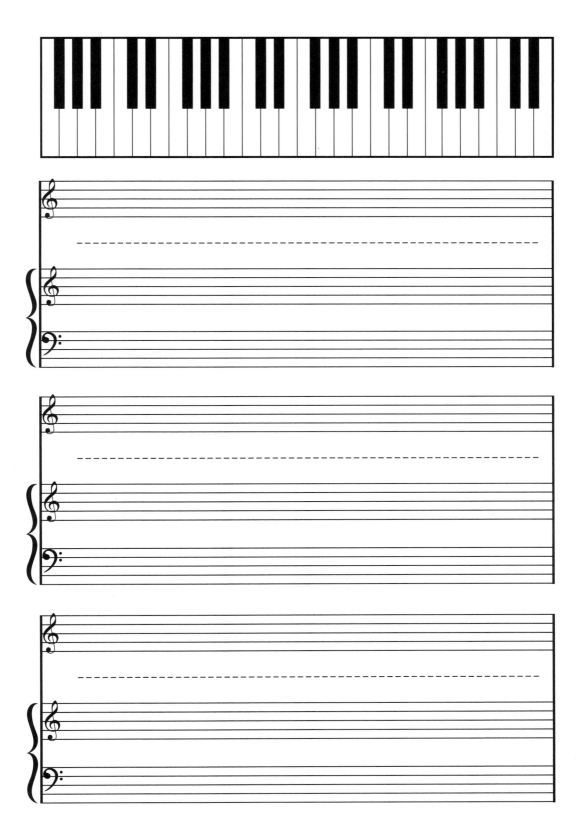

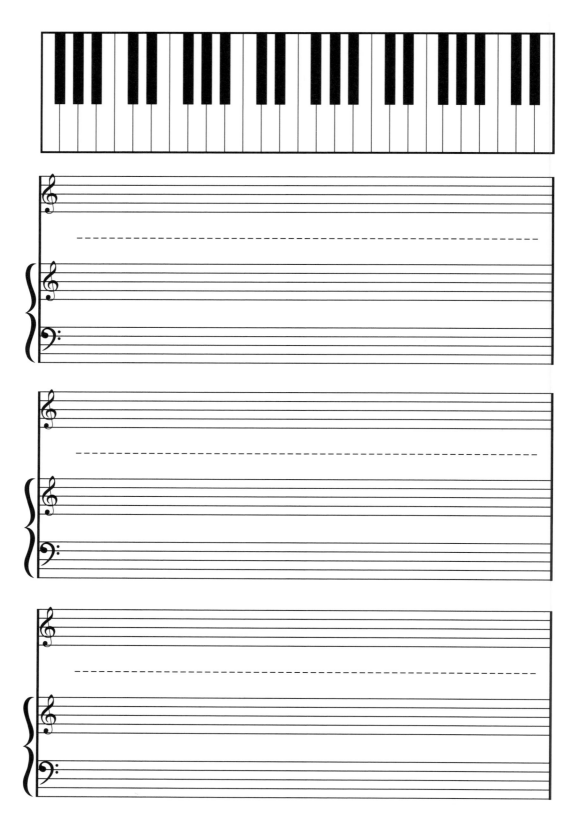

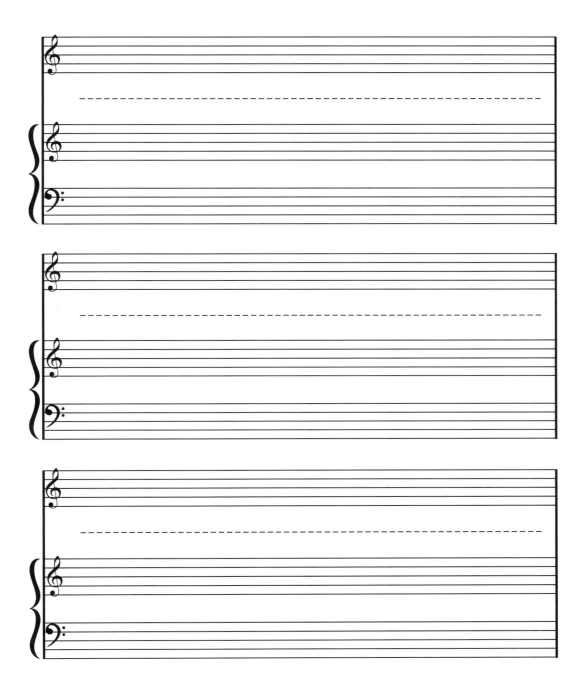

It's an annoyance sometimes. You get an idea for a song,
a piece of music, a piano piece, an orchestral piece —
at the most inopportune moment.

KEITH EMERSON

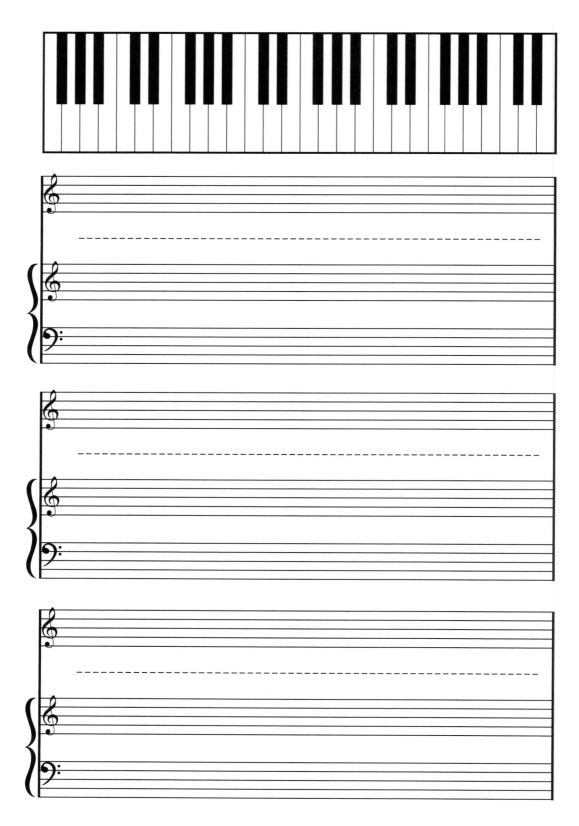

I write pop songs. But I think it is sprinkled with a lot of counter-culture references. It ranged from rap to hip hop to trip hop, house, drum and bass, and experimental and improv and jazz.

NELLY FURTADO

Title _____

Author _____

Date _____

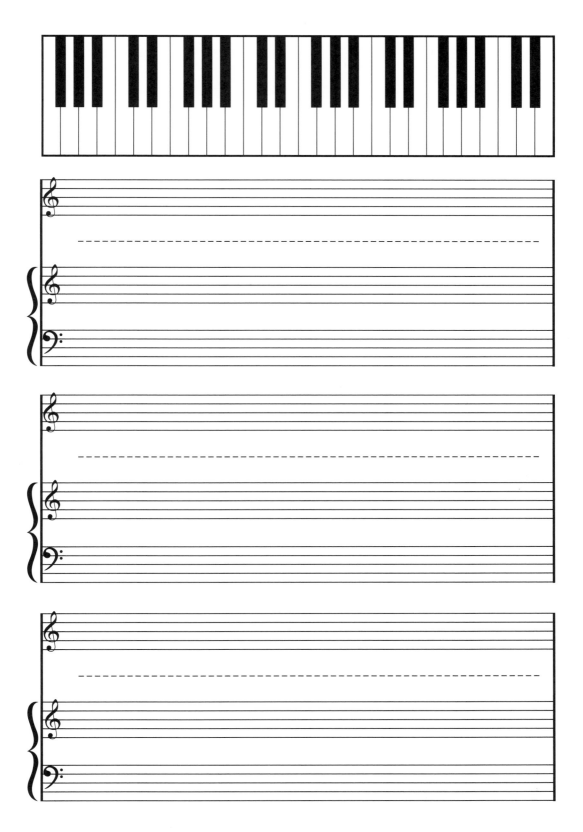

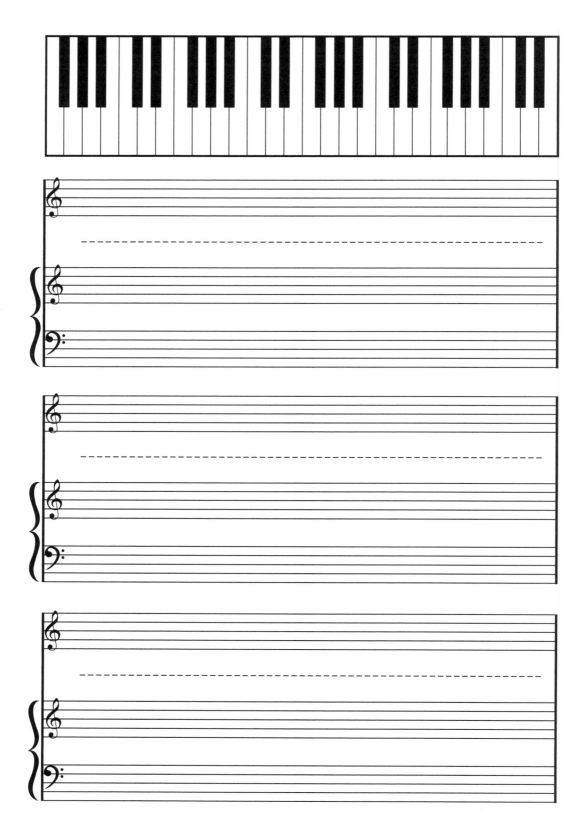

My role in society, or any artist's or poet's role, is to try and
express what we all feel. Not to tell people how to feel. Not as
a preacher, not as a leader, but as a reflection of us all.

JOHN LENNON

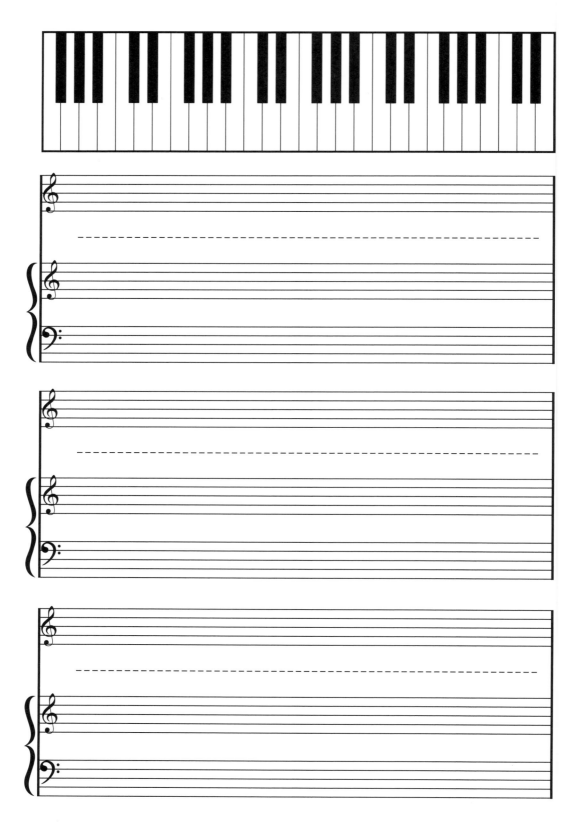

No other acoustic instrument can match
the piano's expressive range, and no electric
instrument can match its mystery.

KENNETH MILLER

Title

Author

Date

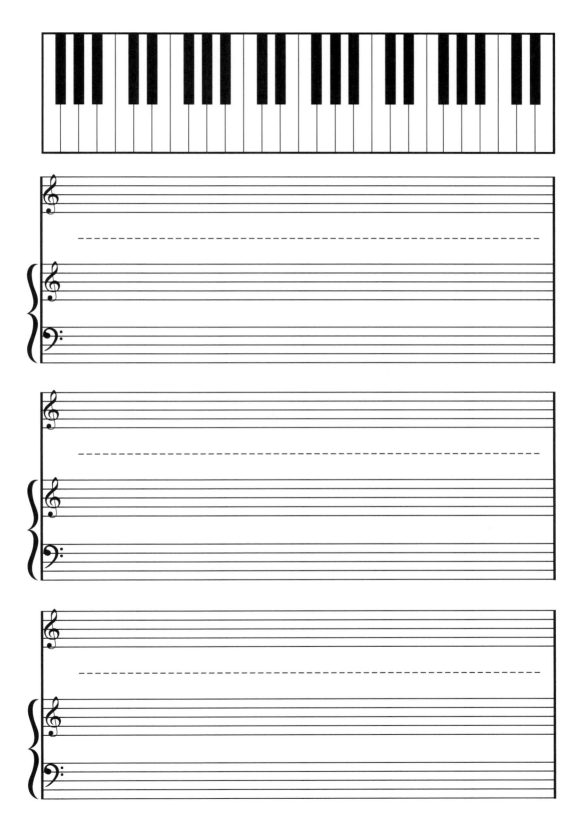

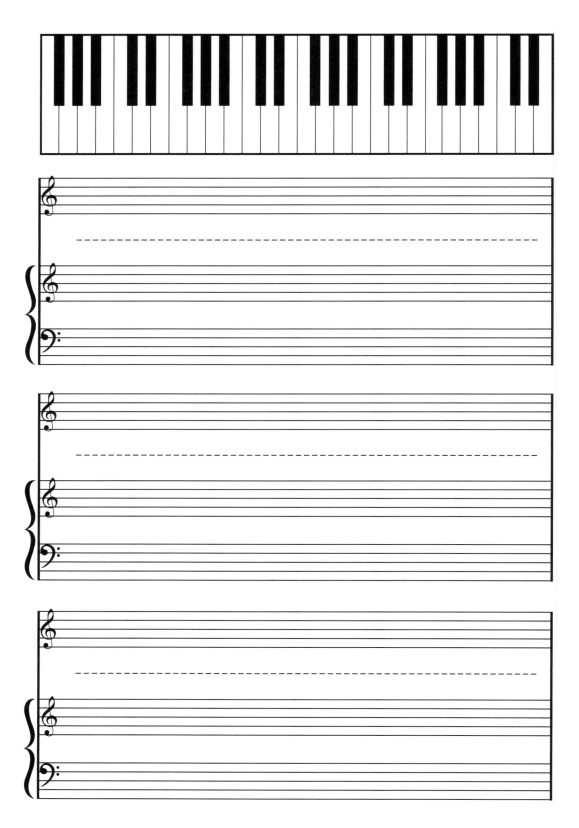

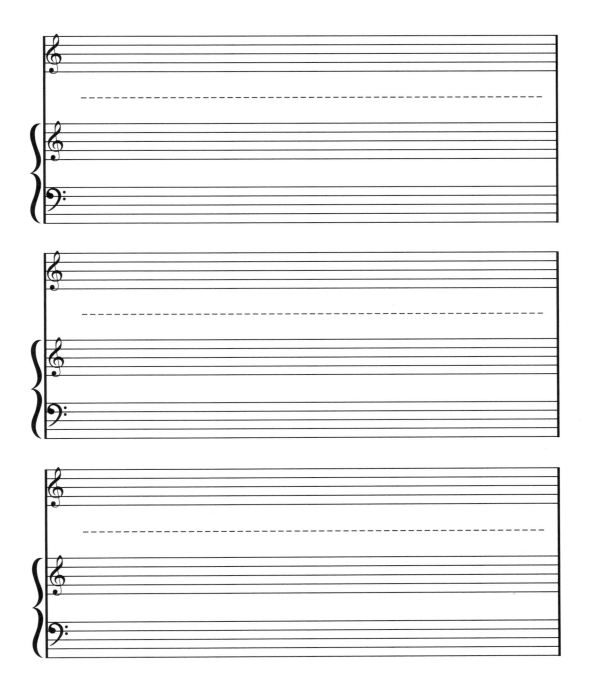

If you develop an ear for sounds that are musical, it is like developing
an ego. You begin to refuse sounds that are not musical and that
way cut yourself off from a good deal of experience.

JOHN CAGE

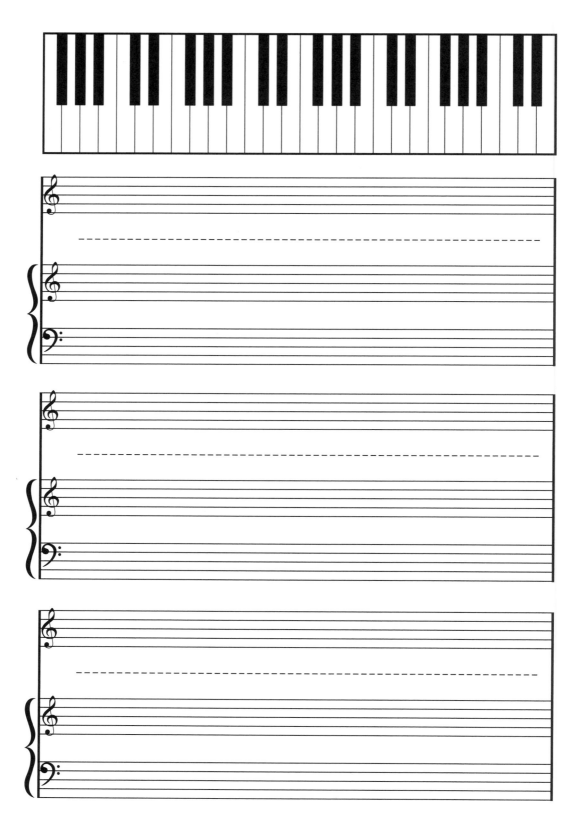

When a pianist sits down and does a virtuoso performance he is in
a technical sense transmitting more information to a machine
than any other human activity involving machinery allows.

ROBERT MOOG

Title _____

Author _____

Date _____

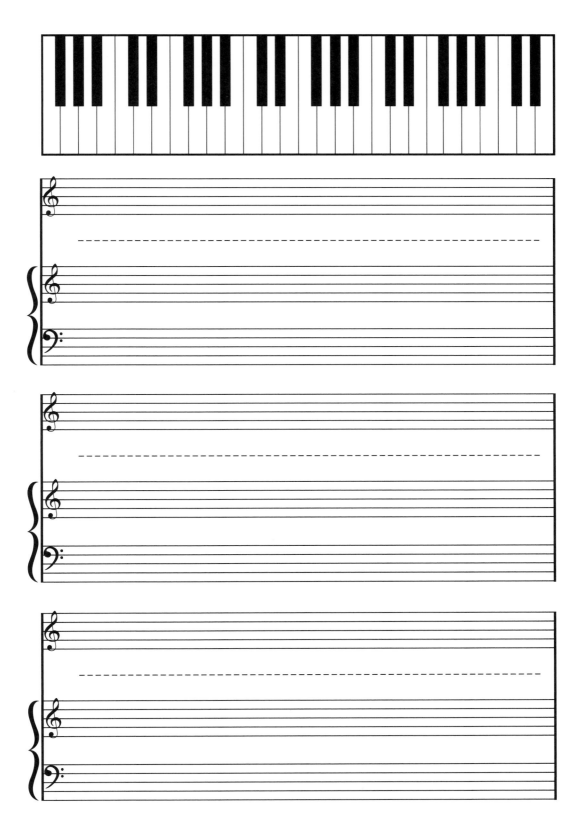

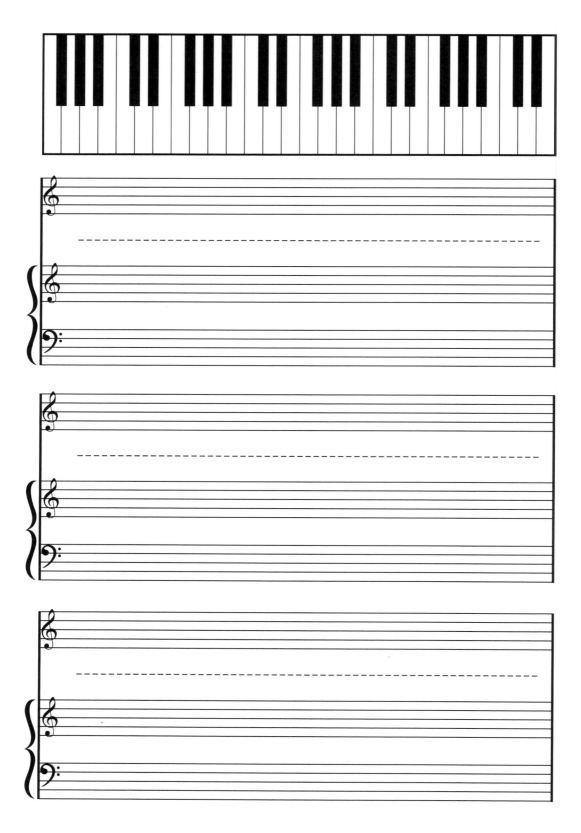

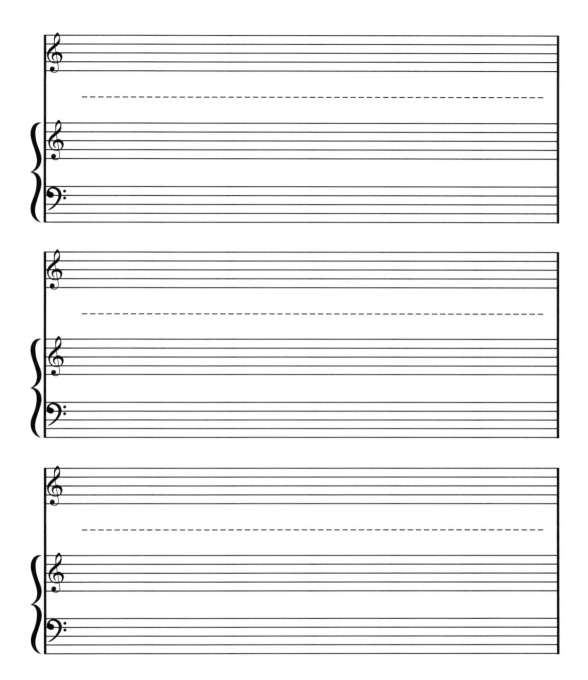

As a pianist I listened to Pinetop Smith, Meade Lux Lewis,
and Albert Ammons and copied them. Then I started
listening to Art Tatum and copying him.

GEORGE SHEARING

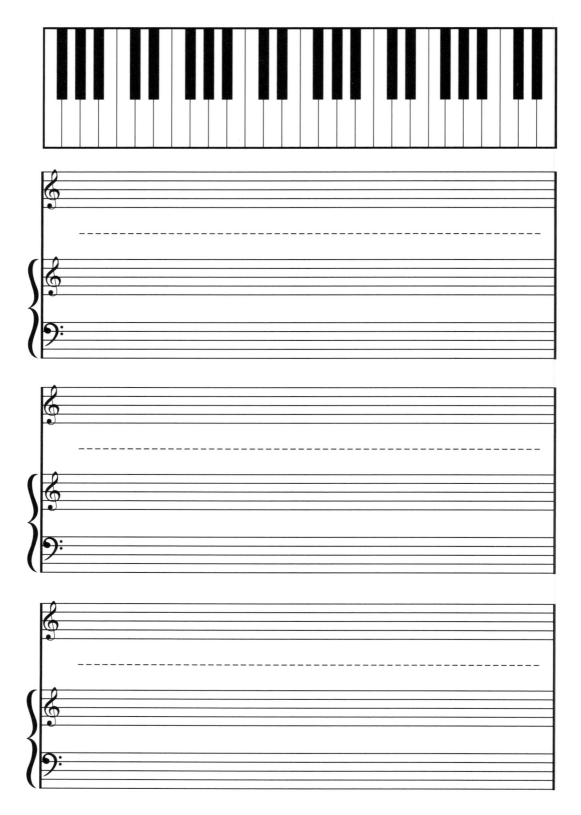

Once I understood Bach's music, I wanted to be a concert pianist.
Bach made me dedicate my life to music, and it was
that teacher who introduced me to his world.

NINA SIMONE

Title

Author

Date

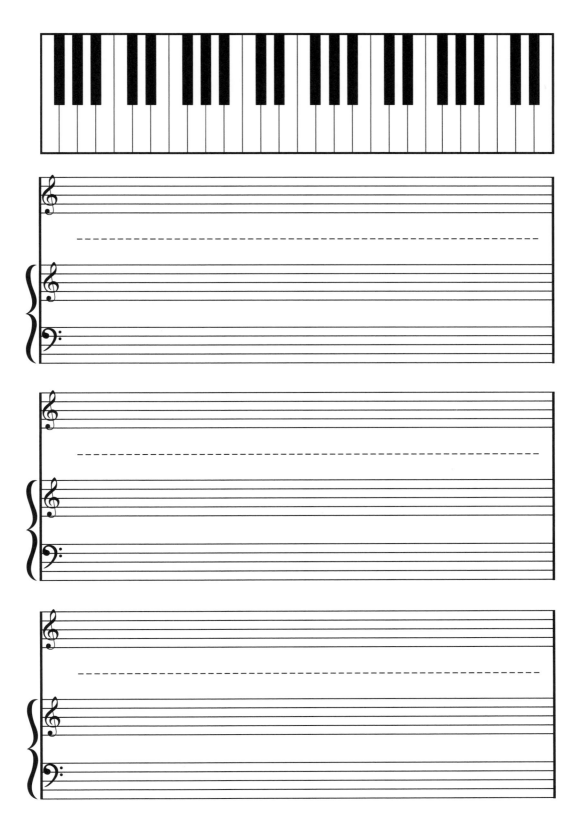

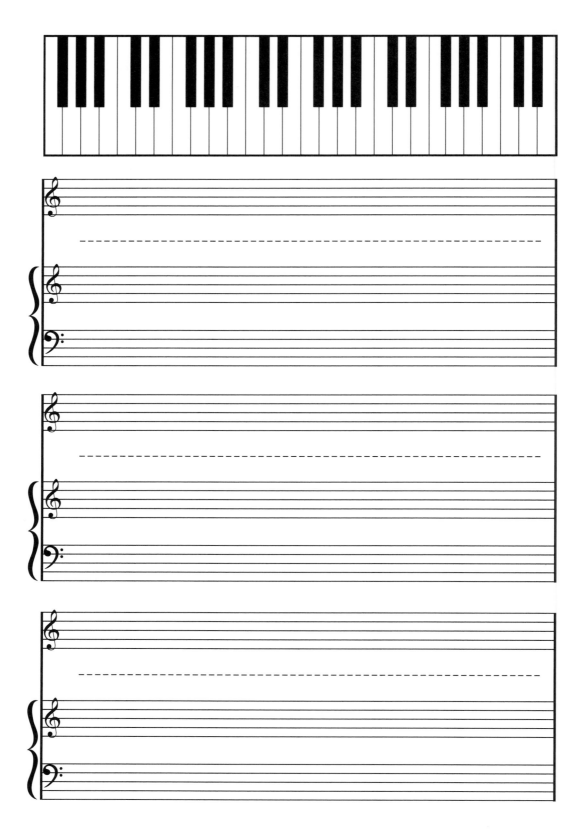

I feel every songwriter should attempt to represent the era in which he or she lives, and we're in an era where the world is entering puberty, which, of course, means that it is overdramatic and awkward.

RUFUS WAINWRIGHT

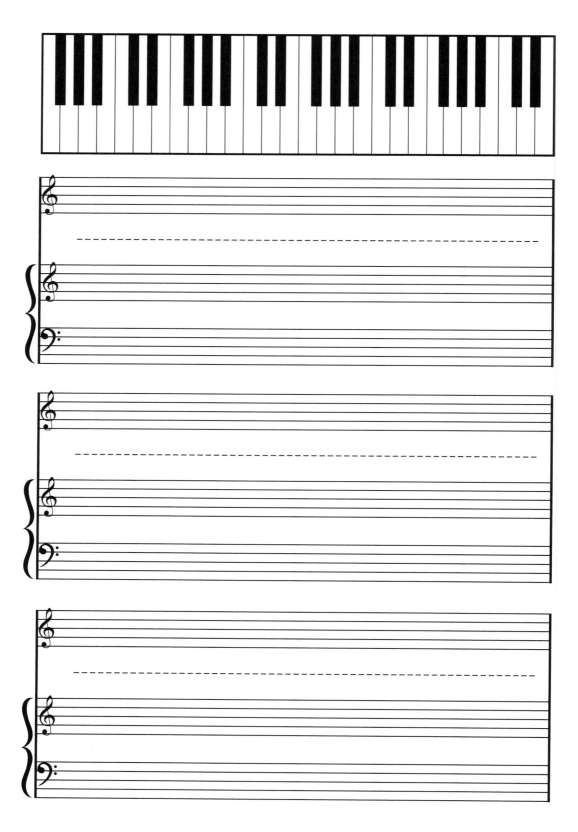

I look at myself as more of a writer than an actual performer. I can't play the piano fast. I'm no Oscar Peterson and I can't read music.

RICHARD WRIGHT

Title

Author

Date

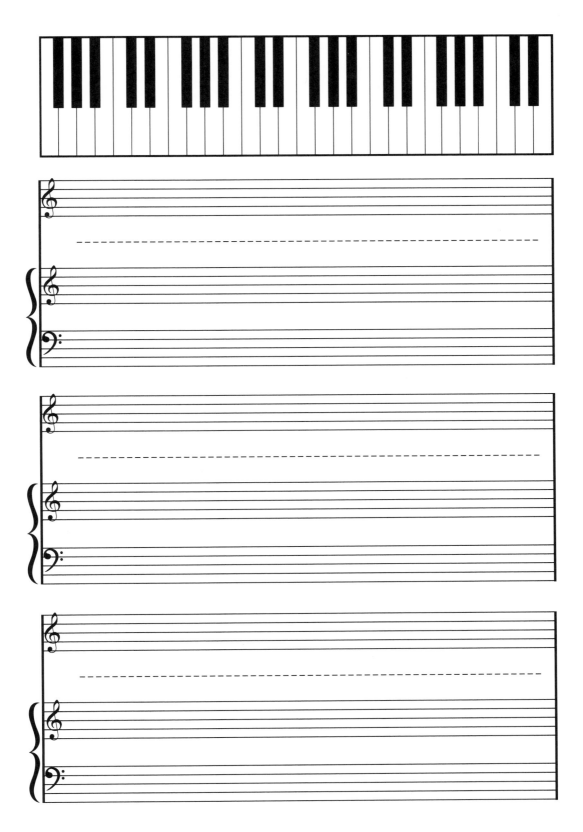

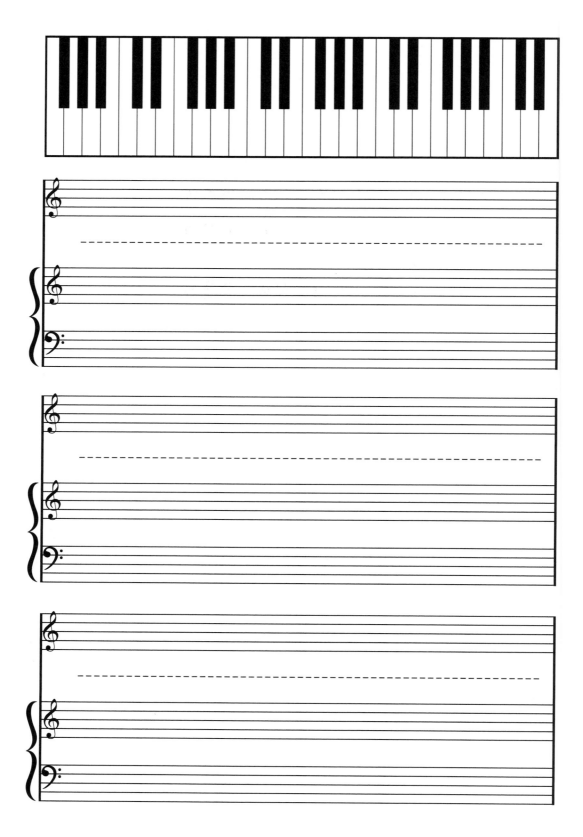

Playing the keyboards is a very competitive business, and if you're going to be in it, you should be able to read and transcribe.

GARTH HUDSON

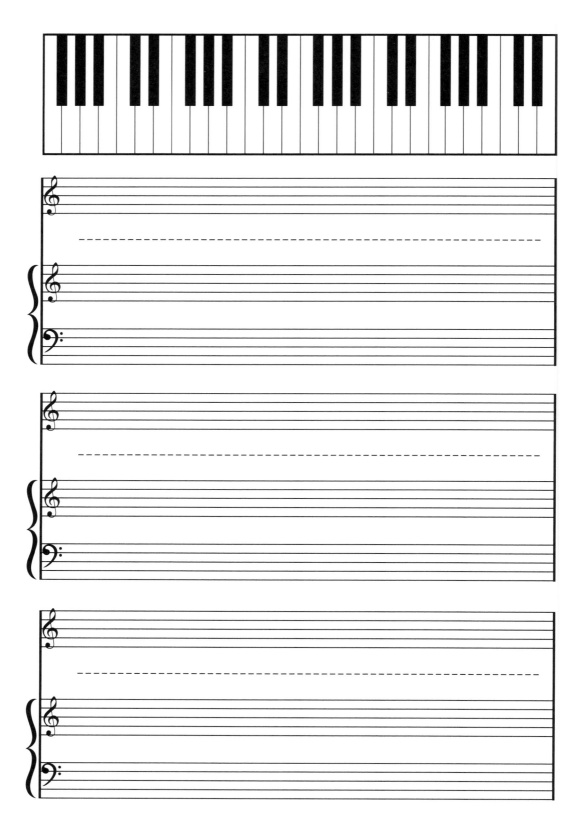

Simplicity is the final achievement. After one has played
a vast quantity of notes and more notes, it is simplicity
that emerges as the crowning reward of art.

FREDERIC CHOPIN

Title

Author

Date

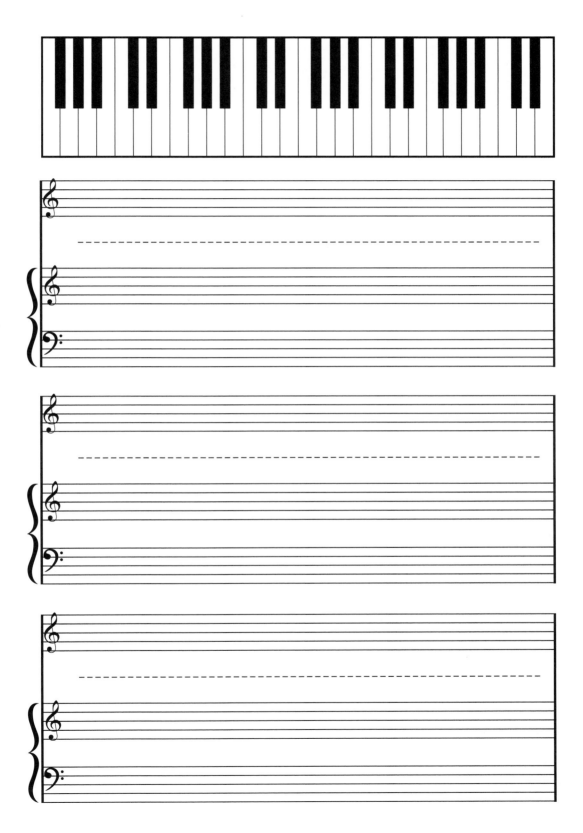

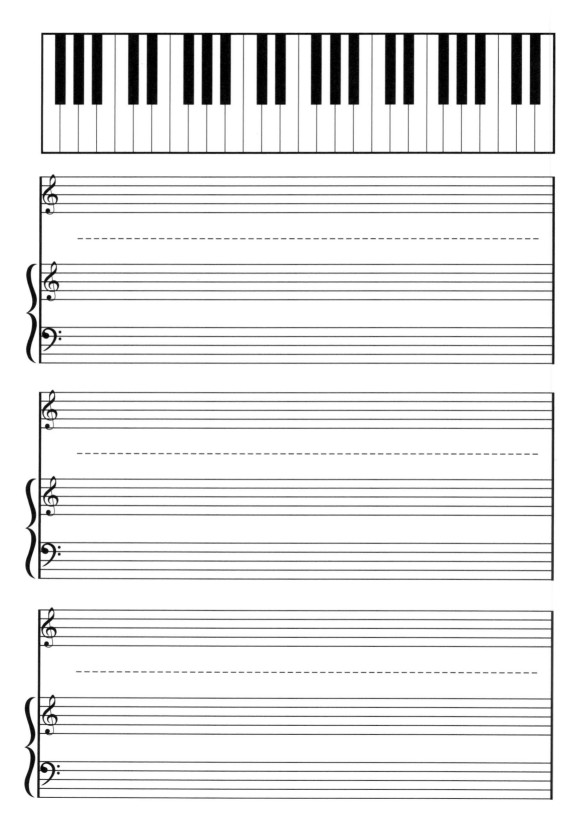

You have to practice improvisation, let no one kid you about it!

ART TATUM

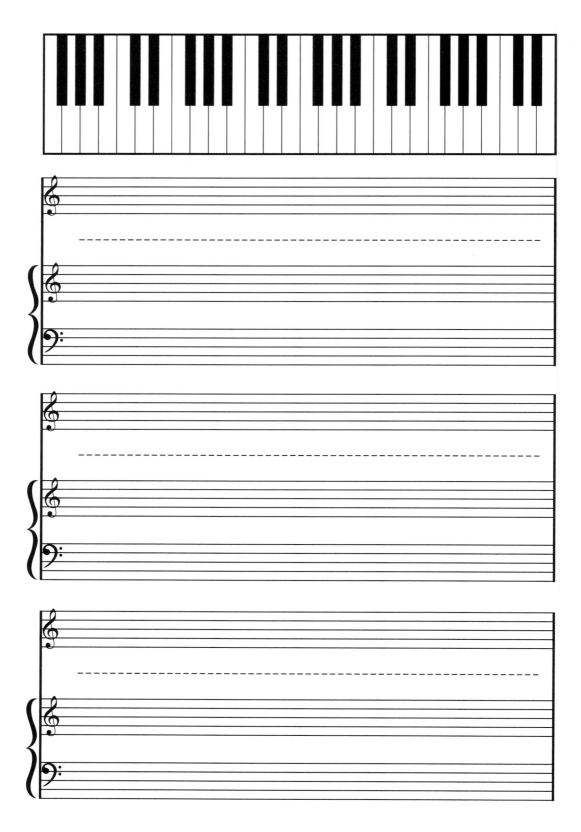

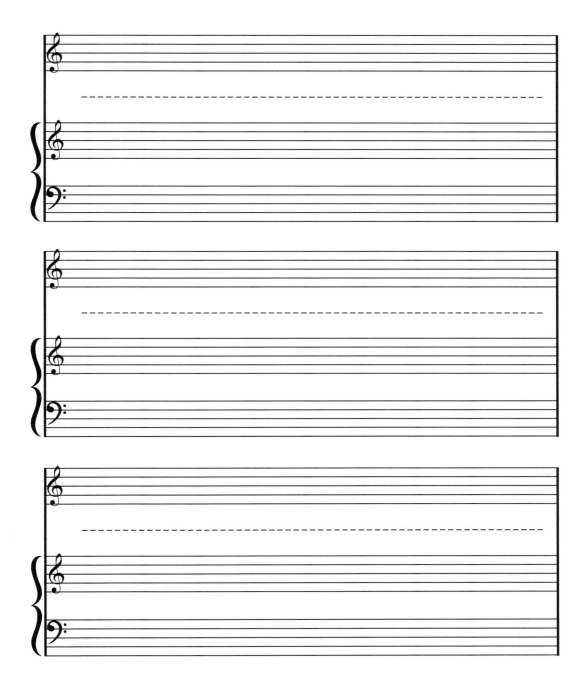

Too many pieces of music finish
too long after the end.

IGOR STRAVINSKY

Title _____

Author _____

Date _____

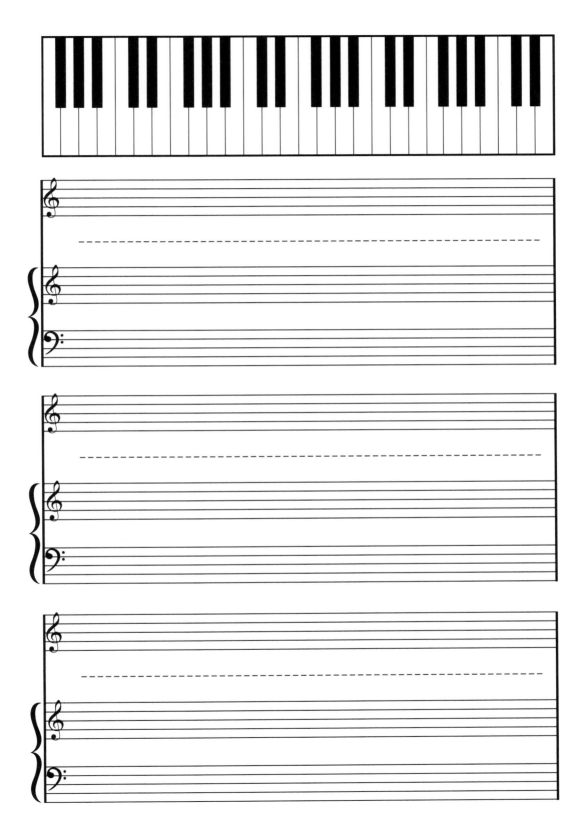

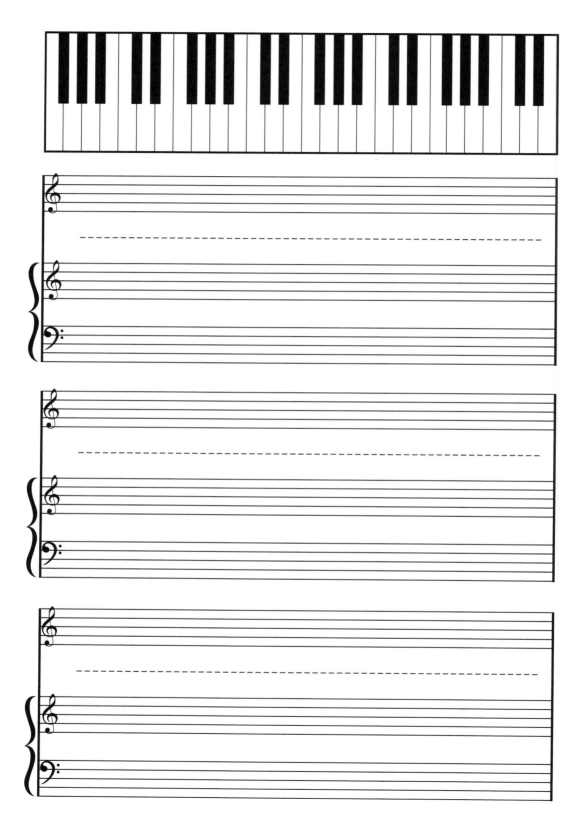

Beware the lollipop of mediocrity;
lick it once and you'll suck forever.

BRIAN WILSON

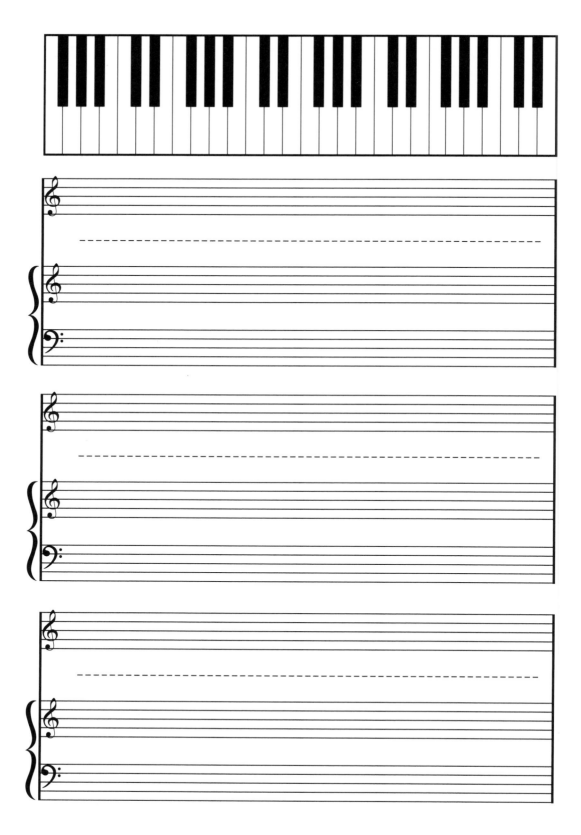

Sometimes when I sit down to practice and there is no one else in
the room, I have to stifle an impulse to ring for the elevator man
and offer him money to come in and hear me.

ARTHUR RUBINSTEIN

Title

Author

Date

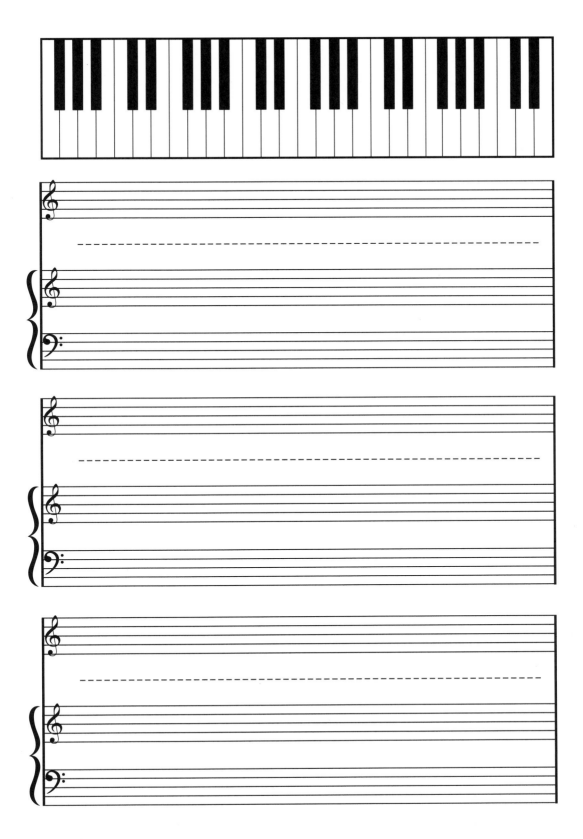

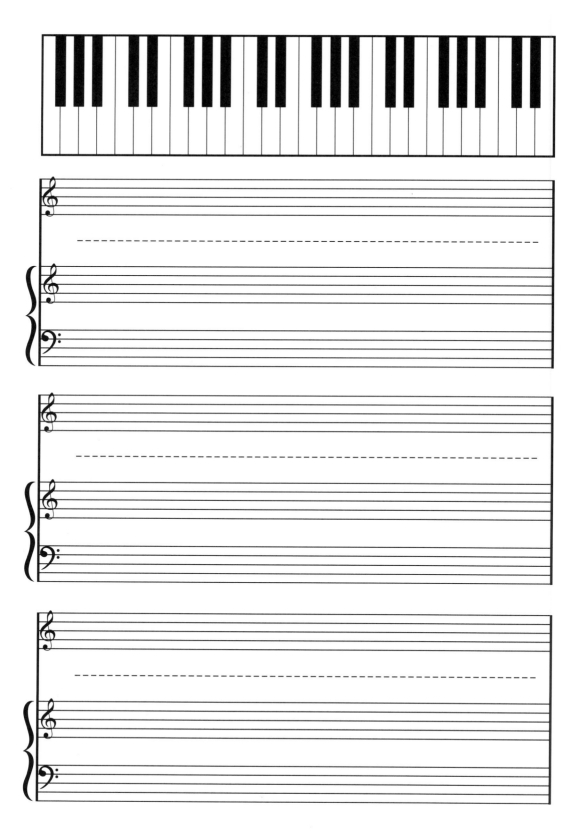

To achieve great things, two things are needed:
a plan, and not quite enough time.

LEONARD BERNSTEIN

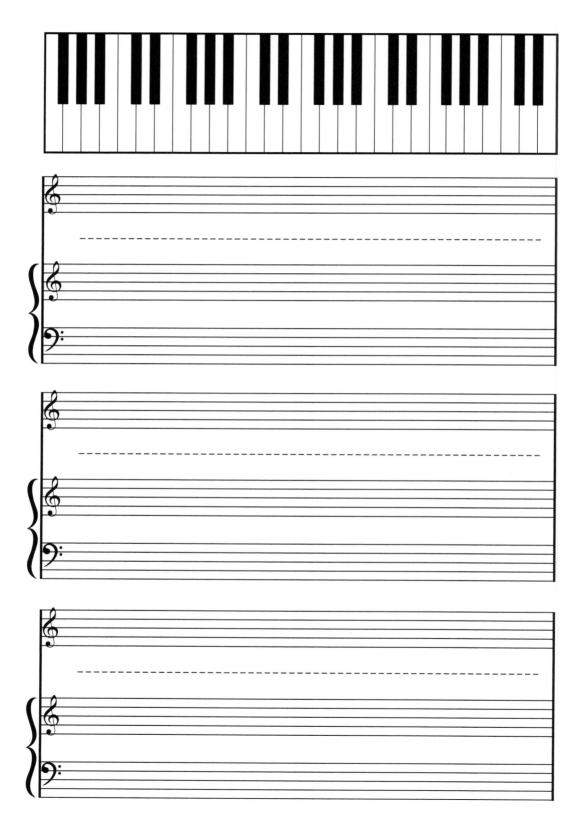

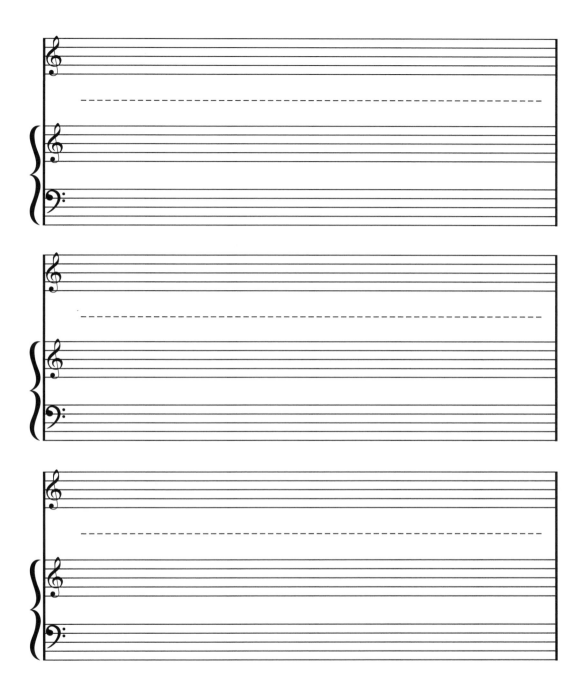

Sometimes it's to your advantage for
people to think you're crazy.

THELONIOUS MONK

Title

Author

Date

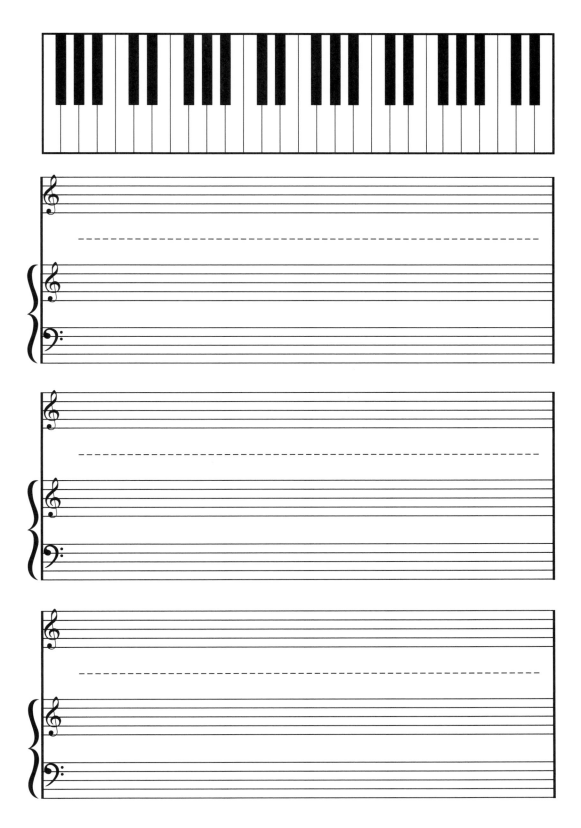

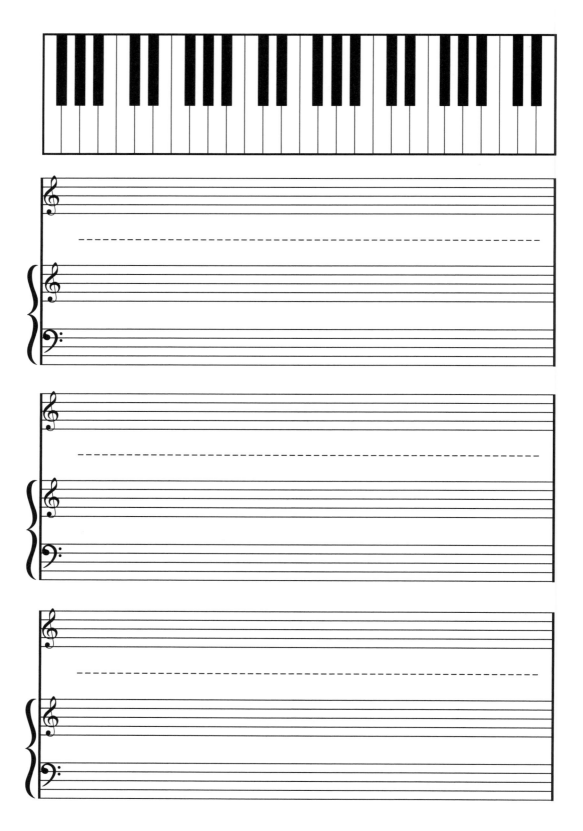

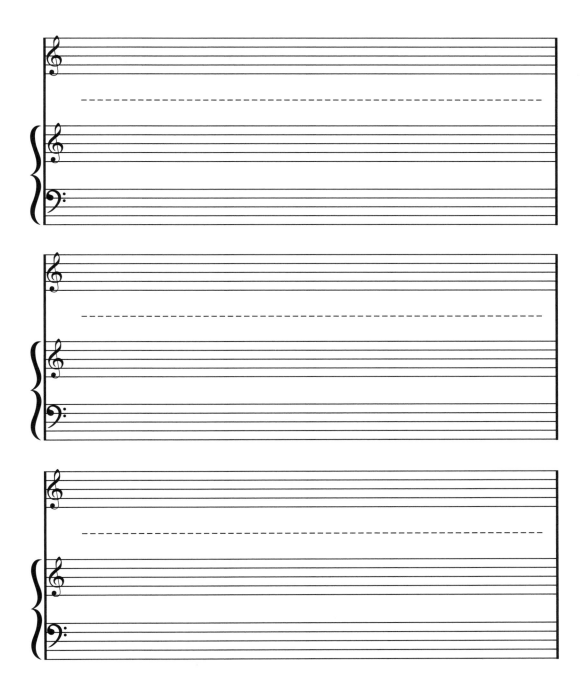

I believe my music can make the blind see, the lame walk, the deaf
and dumb hear and talk because it inspires and uplifts people.

LITTLE RICHARD

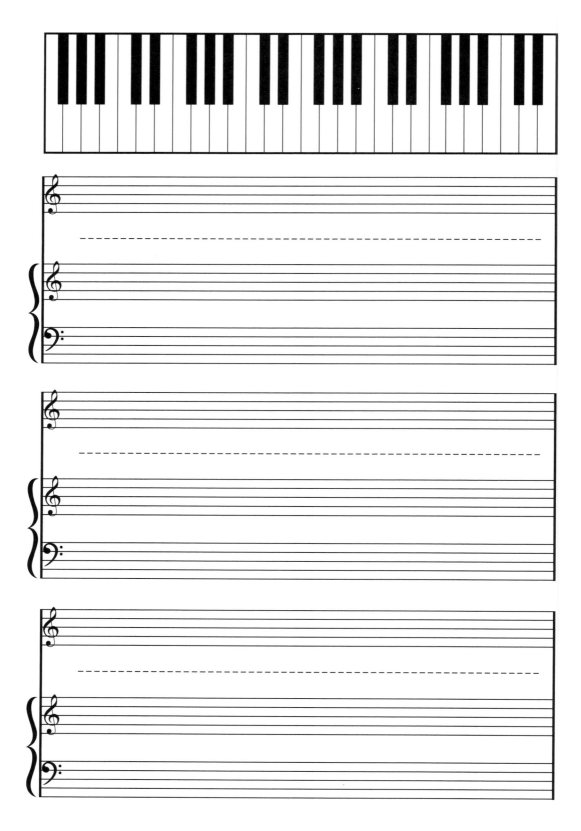

I love the piano. There's a certain sound it adds to a record that feels really good. It's really crisp, and it has a classic feel.

JOHN LEGEND

Title

Author

Date

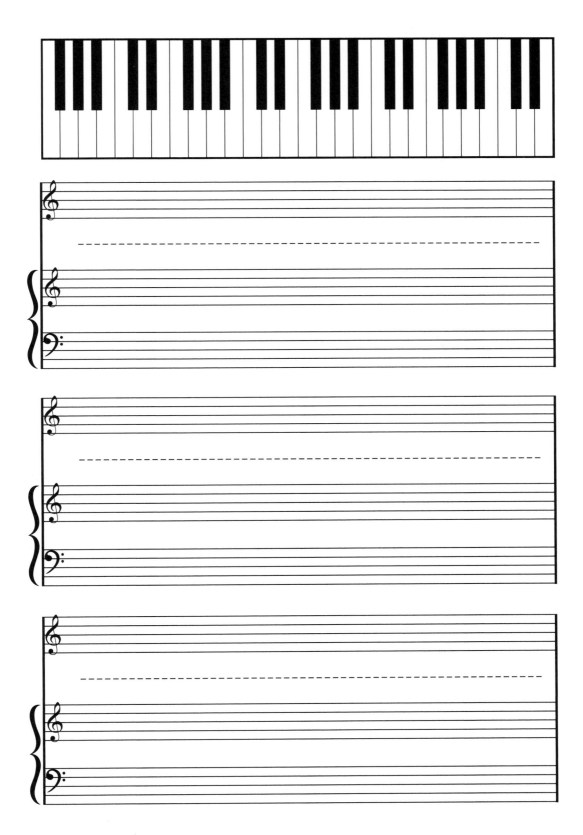

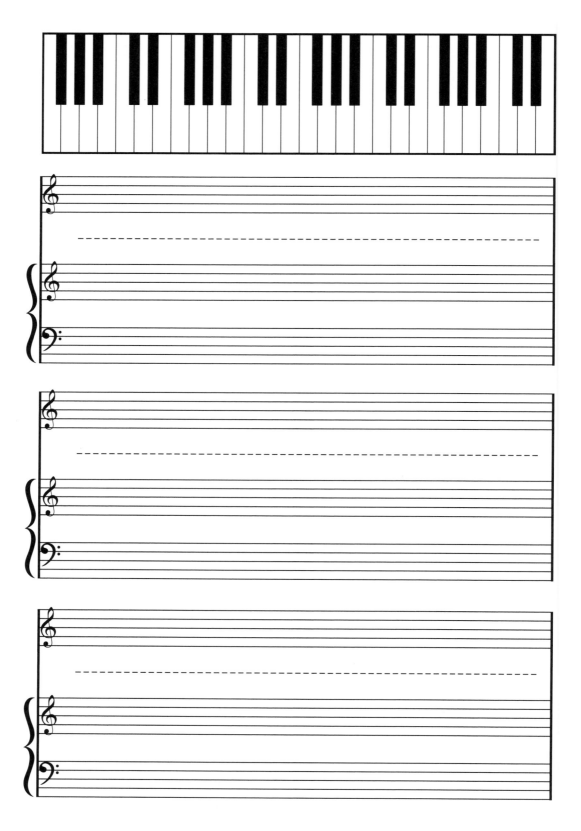

I was at high school when my first big chance came along.
Hits and Bits, a traveling TOBA show, had just hit town,
and the pianist had failed to show up.

MARY LOU WILLIAMS

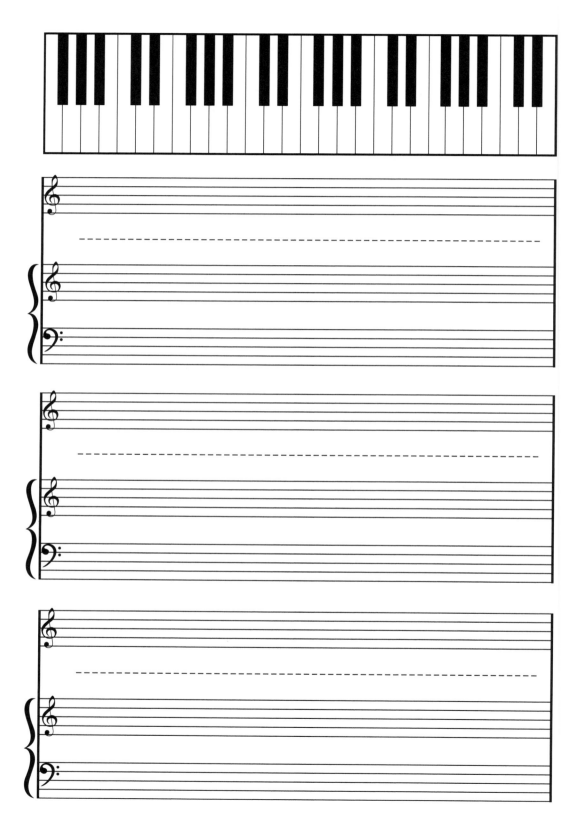

People compose for many reasons: to become immortal;
because they have looked into a pair of beautiful eyes;
for no reason whatsoever.

ROBERT SCHUMANN

Title _____

Author _____

Date _____

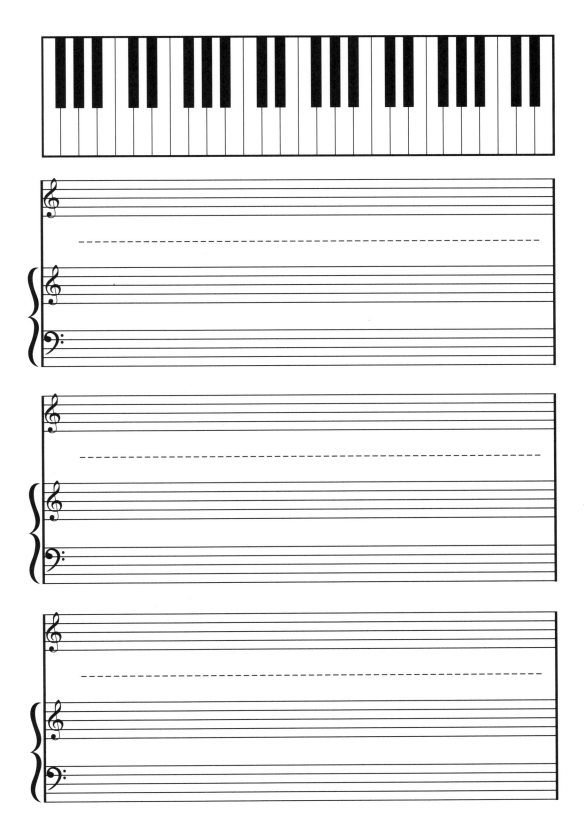

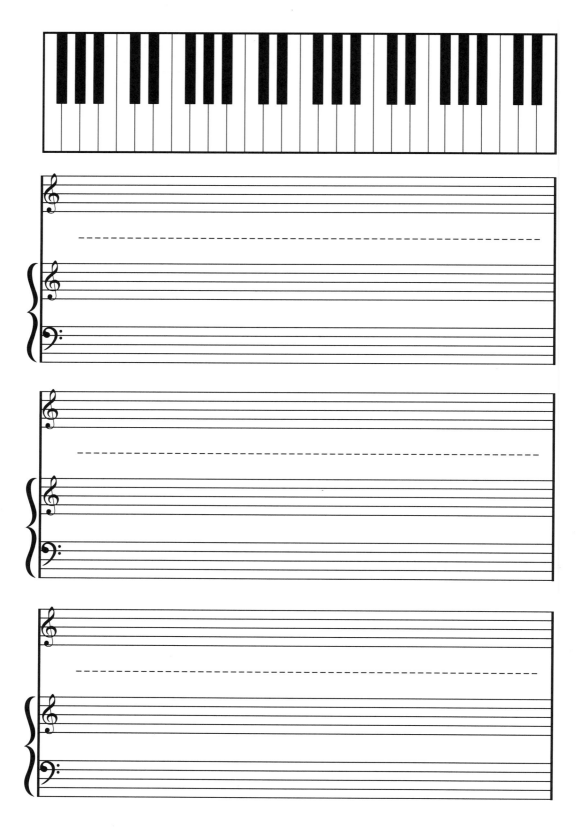

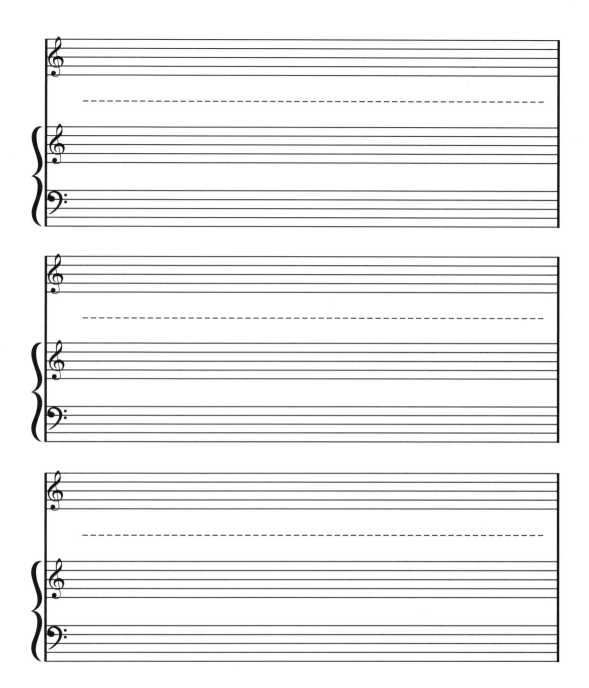

Be nice to people on your way up because
you meet them on your way down.

JIMMY DURANTE

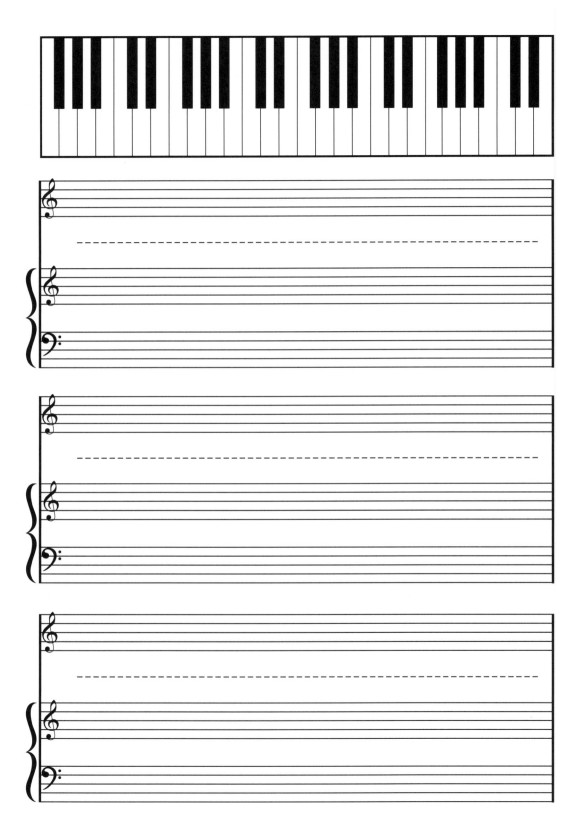

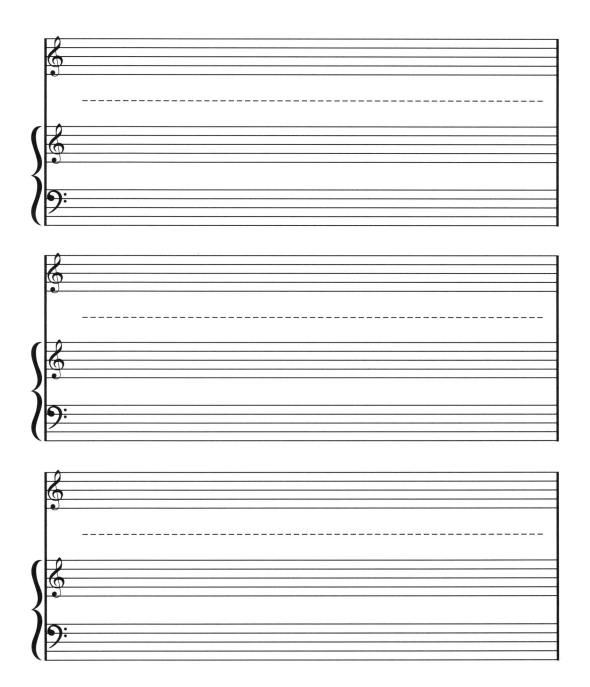

I don't usually write when I'm in a good mood.
That's when I want to be out living a life.

DANIEL JOHNS

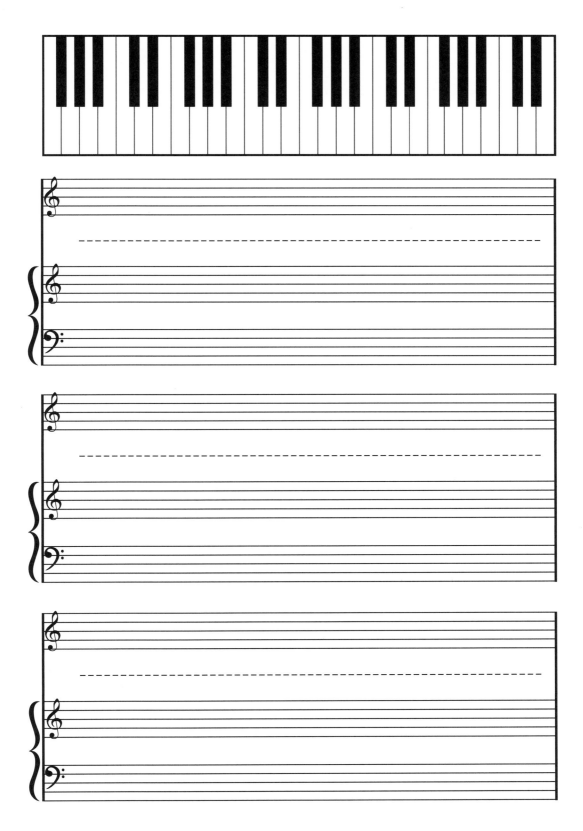

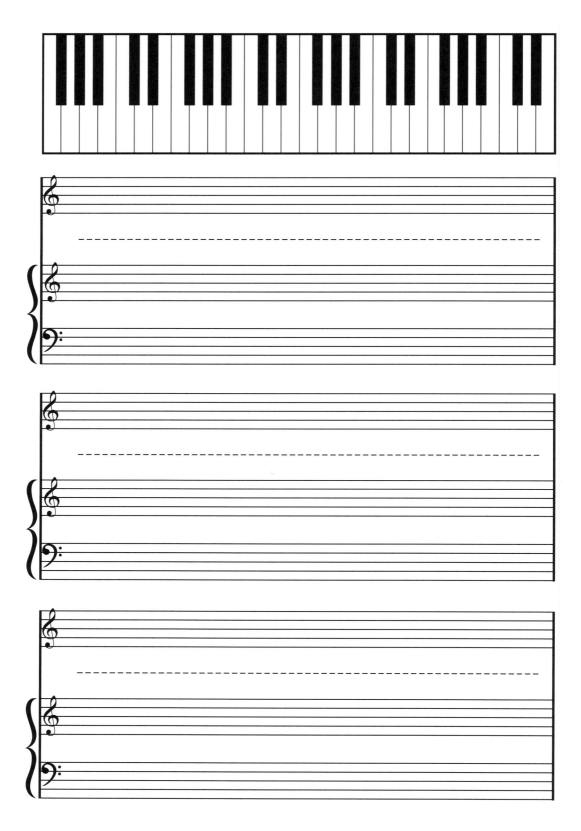

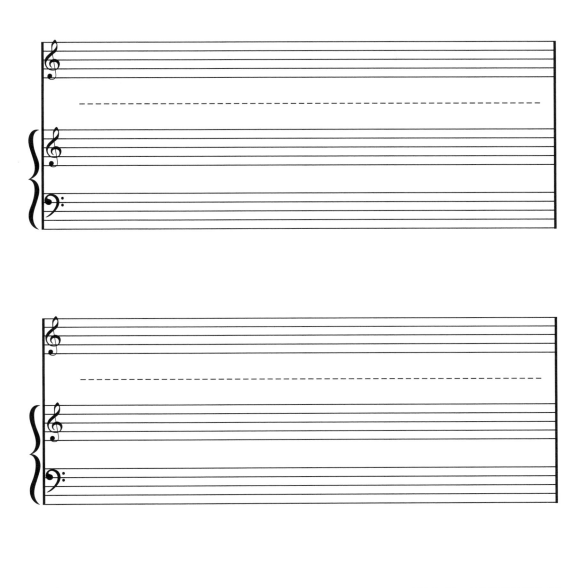

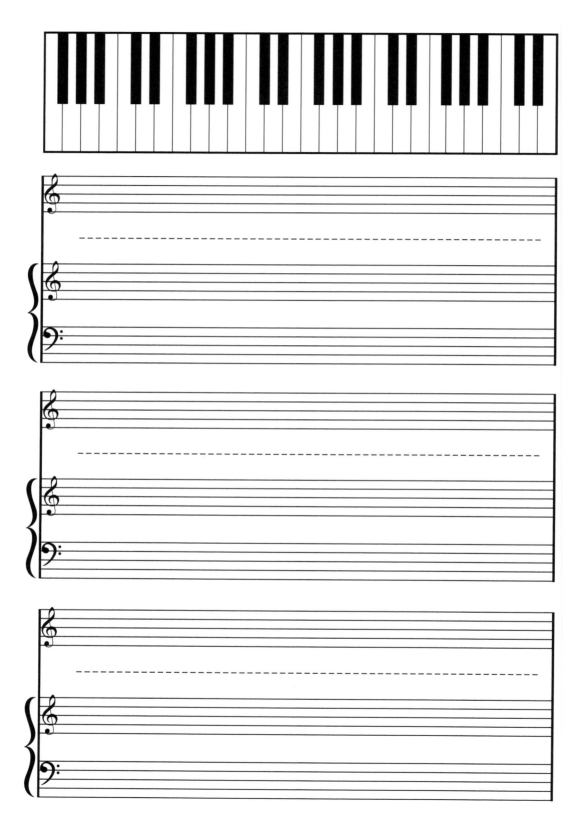

Chords, scales, & arpeggios

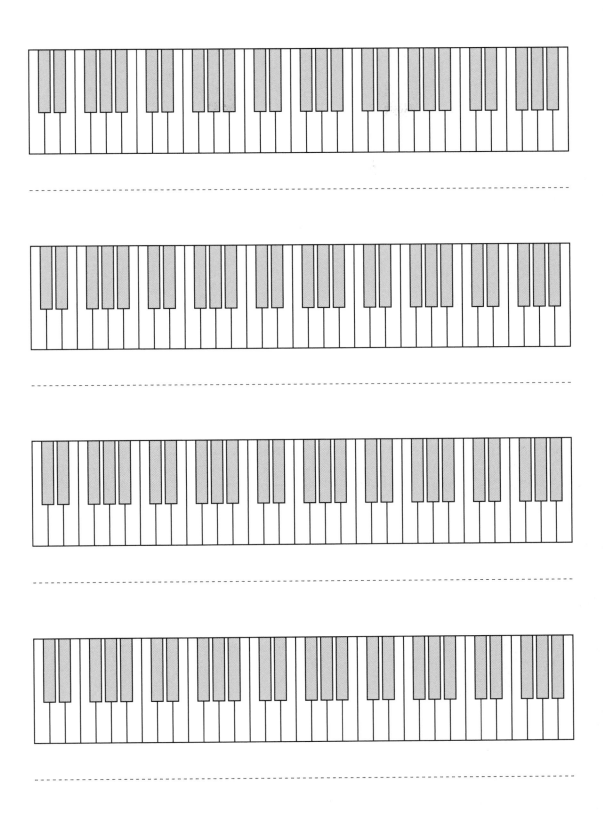

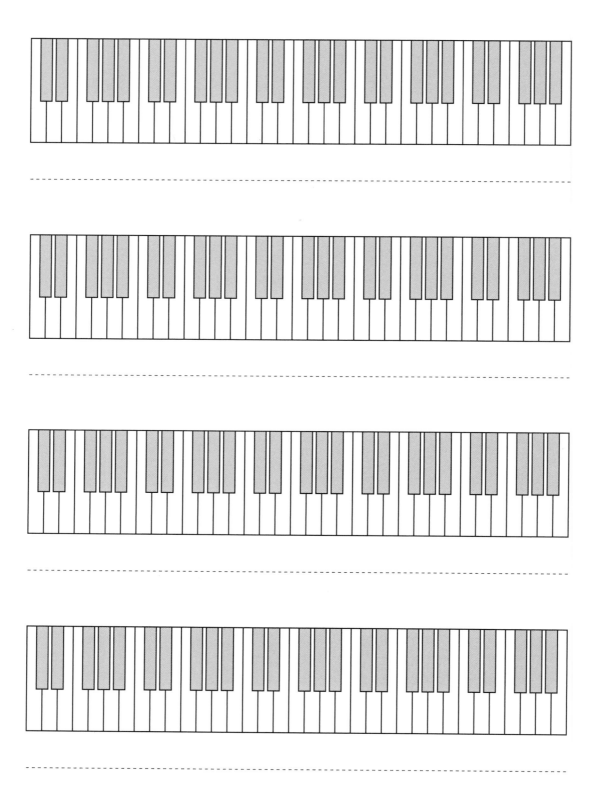

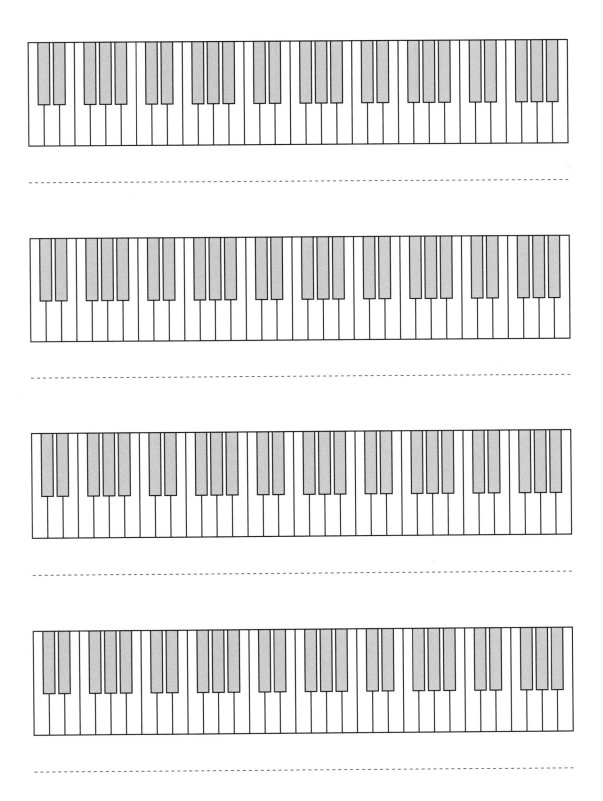

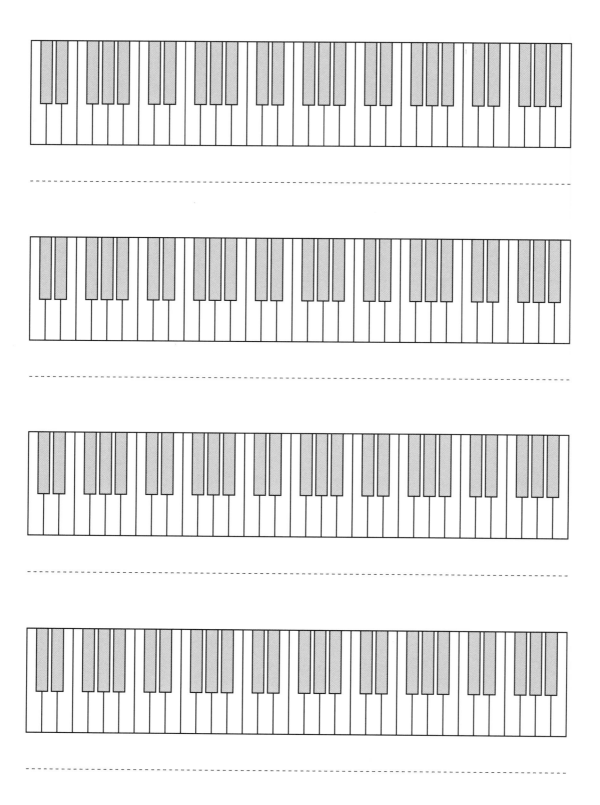

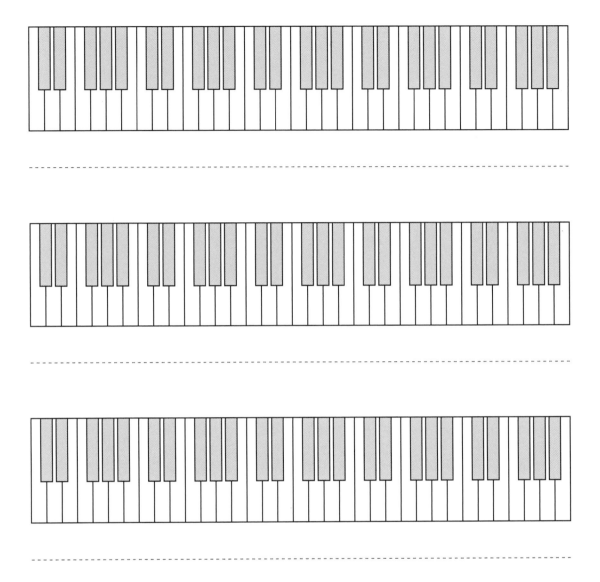

If you have any suggestions on how to make this journal more useful please write to
Matt@sinestudios.com.

About Cider Mill Press
Book Publishers

Good ideas ripen with time. From seed to harvest, Cider Mill Press brings fine reading, information, and entertainment together between the covers of its creatively crafted books. Our Cider Mill bears fruit twice a year, publishing a new crop of titles each spring and fall.

Visit us on the Web at
www.cidermillpress.com
or write to us at
12 Port Farm Road
Kennebunkport, Maine 04046